# What became of the Bones of St Thomas?

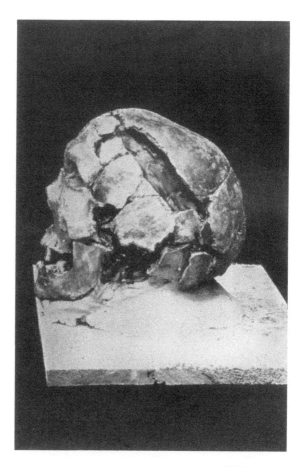

THE SKULL FOUND IN 1888

# What became of the Bones of St Thomas?

## A CONTRIBUTION TO HIS FIFTEENTH JUBILEE

BY

ARTHUR JAMES MASON, D.D.

CANON OF CANTERBURY

CAMBRIDGE
AT THE UNIVERSITY PRESS
1920

CAMBRIDGE UNIVERSITY PRESS
Cambridge, New York, Melbourne, Madrid, Cape Town,
Singapore, São Paulo, Delhi, Tokyo, Mexico City

Cambridge University Press
The Edinburgh Building, Cambridge CB2 8RU, UK

Published in the United States of America by
Cambridge University Press, New York

www.cambridge.org
Information on this title: www.cambridge.org/9781107600478

© Cambridge University Press 1920

First published 1920
First paperback edition 2011

*A catalogue record for this publication is available from the British Library*

ISBN 978-1-107-60047-8 Paperback

# PREFACE

HIS GRACE the present Archbishop of Canterbury some time ago expressed to me the wish that I would put together the documents bearing on the question whether the bones discovered in 1888 were those of his great predecessor or not. He was good enough to desire that my book on the *Mission of St Augustine* (Cambridge, 1897) should be taken as the model—that is, that the reader should have before him the documentary evidence in such a form as to be able to draw his own conclusions. This I have endeavoured to the best of my ability to do. To a certain extent I have departed from the model, in not giving the original everywhere in full, where a document is translated from the Latin. In the present shortage of paper it seemed wasteful to print many pages of Latin matter which is easily accessible to students, as in the case of the narratives of the Passion, or of Erasmus's *Colloquies*. The work has been delayed by many interruptions, but it is now issued in good time for the "Jubilee of St Thomas,"—the fourteenth Jubilee of the Translation, the fifteenth of the Martyrdom.

Besides my obligations to printed sources of information, I owe thanks for assistance of various kinds to many generous helpers; to the Dean of Wells for the elucidation of some difficulties in interpreting the narratives of the Passion; to Professors Sir Clifford Allbutt and Macalister in reference to mediaeval histology; to Professor Breul and Mr E. G. W. Braunholtz for help with documents in mediaeval German and French; to the Rev. C. E. Woodruff in dealing with the records contained in our own Library; to Mr D. T. Baird Wood for help in connexion with papers in the British Museum, especially with Sir R. Cotton's description of the shrine; to Mr C. Hilary Jenkinson for kindly aid at the Record Office; to Professor A. F. Pollard and Miss E. Jeffries Davis for answers to enquiries relating to matters in the reign of Henry VIII; to Monsignor G. Mercati, who, with his proverbial kindness, replied to a simple question about R. Hilliard by going into the whole relation between Hilliard, Sanders, Pollini, and Henriquez, as if the subject were on his own chosen ground of studies; to Mrs Bolton and Sister Lisa Rawlinson for the vivid letters describing the discovery in 1888; to Mr J. McClemens and Mr S. Caldwell for many things connected with the cathedral building and the windows; to Mr Charlton of Mercery Lane, Canterbury, for leave to reproduce his photograph of the skull; and beyond all to Mr W. D. Caroe, who in the midst of all his professional labours found time to make me the plan of the buildings to explain the story of the Martyrdom.

Whether the general verdict upon this collection proves to be in favour of assigning these bones to St Thomas or not, I hope that the book may serve as a tribute of admiration to a great man and a great champion of religious liberty, in the form in which his age understood it.

A. J. M.

*Allhallowmas*, 1919

# CONTENTS

## SECTION I

### THE NARRATIVES OF THE PASSION

## SECTION II

### THE TOMB AND THE SHRINE

## SECTION III

### THE DESTRUCTION OF THE SHRINE

## SECTION IV

### THE SUPPOSED DISCOVERY OF THE BONES

## BOOKS OFTEN REFERRED TO IN THESE PAGES.

"Materials" = *Materials for the History of Archbishop Thomas Becket*, by J. C. Robertson (Rolls Series, 1875 and subsequent years).

"Garnier" = Garnier de Pont St Maxence, ed. C. Hippeau (Paris, 1859).

Thómas Saga Erkibyskups, ed. E. Magnússon (Rolls Series).

R. Willis, *The Architectural History of Canterbury Cathedral*, 1845.

— *The Architectural History of the Conventual Buildings of the Monastery of Christ Church in Canterbury*, 1869.

"Stanley" = *Historical Memorials of Canterbury*, by Arthur P. Stanley (12th edition, 1891).

"Inventories" = *Inventories of Christchurch Canterbury*, by J. Wickham Legg and W. H. St John Hope (1902).

"Scott Robertson" = *The Crypt of Canterbury Cathedral*, by W. A. Scott Robertson (1880).

# SECTION I

## THE NARRATIVES OF THE PASSION

# SECTION I

## THE NARRATIVES OF THE PASSION

THE first step towards determining whether the bones discovered in 1888 are or are not the bones of St Thomas must be to consider the original records of the martyrdom, and see whether they give any clear indication of the nature of the wound or wounds received by the Archbishop.

Five men who were present during the last hours of St Thomas have left us their accounts of what took place. The five are William of Canterbury, a monk of the convent at the time; William Fitzstephen, a clerk in attendance on the Archbishop; Benedict, one of the monks, afterwards Abbot of Peterborough; the celebrated John of Salisbury; and Edward Grim, often described as a monk and crossbearer to the Archbishop, but in reality a clerk from Cambridge who happened to be on a visit to St Thomas. To these may be added a sixth, the historian Gervase, a monk of the cathedral, who was certainly present at the saint's burial, and therefore perhaps at the scene of the day before; but Gervase's narrative as a whole need not be printed here, as it consists only of a combination of sentences from the accounts given by others before him. One passage of Gervase, however, concerning the wounded head, is of great importance, and must be carefully studied.

It is not easy to be sure of the order in which the five witnesses gave their accounts to the world, or to say how far they were dependent upon each other or upon reports current in their time. The two narratives which give the impression of the greatest freshness and independence are those of the two Williams. Edward Grim, who might have been expected to stand highest of all, is somewhat disappointing. He wrote later than Benedict, to whose work he explicitly refers.

Probably the French poem of Garnier de Pont St Maxence was published earlier than any of the accounts given by these eye-witnesses. Garnier was not himself an eye-witness, but he came to Canterbury to make enquiries within two years of the martyrdom, and finished his work in two years more. His story is, therefore, a good summary of local opinion and belief within a very short time from the event.

The omissions which I have indicated by dots are for the most part edifying reflexions which do not bear upon the present purpose. I have however inserted the narratives at greater than strictly necessary length, partly for their intrinsic interest, partly that the reader may have some means of comparing their value as historical records.

## (1) WILLIAM OF CANTERBURY.

*(Materials for the History of Thomas Becket*, Rolls Series, Vol. 1. p. 129.)

These four then, on their arrival, asked for an interview with the primate. "Do you wish it to be in public," he asked, "or in private?" They answered, "As you please." They withdrew into the inner part of the house, and the servants were sent away; but just as his men were turning to go, the archbishop bethought himself of the saying in the gospel, "Jesus did not commit Himself unto them, because He knew all men." The text seemed to him prophetic of what was coming, and he called them back. Fitzurse then said, "Go to the king, your lord[1], and show yourself in person; you owe it to him as a subject." He replied, "I have done what I ought: I do not remember to have left anything undone that I am in duty bound to do." "No?" they said; "you have not yet absolved the bishops and clergy whom you excommunicated." He rejoined, "The excommunication did not proceed from me." They replied,

[1] I.e. the "young" king, who was in England.

"It is just the same as if it had proceeded from you:—you got it issued." He answered, "I am well satisfied if the patron of the churches[1] avenges the wrongs done to me and to the church which I serve[2]. You, Reginald, were present, and two hundred knights besides, if evidence is wanted, when my lord the king gave me leave to enquire about those who had thrown the church into confusion, and to set right what was amiss and to exact condign satisfaction for presumptuous encroachments. I should in fact be compelled, if the delinquents were not to make reparation, to ask redress for the wrongs which are showered upon me even now. The wine which I brought from abroad by the kindness of my lord the king, and with his warrant, is seized. A horse of mine, in token of contempt for me, as if the maiming of the animal were a disgrace to myself, has been docked of its tail. The churches are still held by intruders." When he had finished the sentence, they answered, "We never heard that leave given to you. But if you wish to complain of wrong done to you, why do you not go to the king and lodge your complaint there? You could have brought it before the nobles, and obtained full satisfaction for the trespass." "I cannot run to court," he said, "for every trifle. The sword of the priesthood must be drawn, when punishment is needed, upon those who require it." At this word they sprang up and shouted, "Threats! threats! Dan[3] monks, we charge you in the king's name, keep this man safe. If he gets away, it will be required at your hands." He answered, "You may be certain that I did not come here to run away, but to abide ·the rage of ruffians and the malice of the wicked. With the favour of God, I care little for your threats." "Not mere threats," they said, "but something more"; and as they rushed away, he followed them all the way to the door and

[1] I.e. the pope.
[2] I.e. the church of Canterbury, whose rights the Archbishop of York had infringed by crowning the young king.
[3] *Domini monachi*: "Dan" is the old English title of courtesy for a monk.

caught by the muttered words of one of them that the king had declared him an outlaw[1].

They determined to do violence to the house; and going out into the court, and bringing in the men whom they had summoned for the purpose, they threw off under a branching mulberry tree, the garments which they had worn over their coats of mail, drew their swords, and flung themselves upon the doors of the outer house, which the servants in terror had barred behind them. Finding themselves repulsed, they put themselves under the guidance of the miserable clerk, Robert, who was acquainted with the secret places of the house. They attacked it from the orchard side, and found the staircase to the postern door interrupted; the builders, who had gone away on some business of their own (as is their way) had left their tools on the spot. These they took to break the bars with. The ladders served them instead of the stairs. There was no one to resist them, and they forced the entrance.

The illustrious champion of God was calmly awaiting the hour of his passion....The exhortations, the prayers, the tears of his friends, could not move him from the spot, until they reminded him that evensong must be said, and laid violent hands upon him, and breaking open a door leading to the cloister, which was bolted, pushed him along, in spite of his resistance.

On reaching the cloister, he moved forward with a slow and measured step, as if he were advancing of his own accord to death. Two servants had run on in front into the midst of the brethren, who were engaged in the service of evensong, and told them more by their terrified bearing than by their words, that the enemy were attacking. Some of the brethren continued at prayers; some sought places of refuge; some desired to give help. One of the brethren stepped outside and said, "Come in, father, come in and

---

[1] Et prosequens usque ad ostium erumpentes deprehendit ad unius mussitationem quia se diffiduciasset rex. "Diffiduciare" means to put him out of the king's "fides" or protection. Cp. Garnier, p. 186: "Et li saint arcevesque disfient bassement."

stay with us, that, if so it must be, we may suffer together and be glorified together. Your absence was death to us; let your presence be our comfort." He replied, "Go, all of you, and fulfil your task of divine service"; and stopping at the church door, he said, "As long as you hold the entrance, I will not go in." They withdrew, and he entered the minster, but stopped on the threshold, and thrusting back the townsfolk who had crowded round him to see the scene, he asked, "What are these people afraid of?" "The armed men in the cloister," was the answer. "I will go out to them," he said. As the brethren would not allow him to do this, he began to pace up and down at the entrance, and being advised to go forward and take his place in the sanctuary, in order that reverence for the spot might procure respect for him, he would not hear of it. Meanwhile the clerks were in a state of agitation, and some of the brethren[1] were placing an iron staple across the door, when he cried, "Begone, you cowards; leave such follies to blind wretches. We charge you on your obedience not to fasten the door."

While he was still speaking, the men at arms, who had been searching the palace, dashed through the cloisters in a body. Three of them held hatchets in their left hands, one of them a double-headed axe; all of them with the right were brandishing drawn swords....As soon as they had sprung through the open door, they parted at the pillar in the middle which supports the vault[2]. Fitzurse took his position to the right, and the three others to the left. The martyr steadfast in mind and body planted himself opposite to them, where it is said that he had once in a dream seen himself crucified; he had on his left hand the cross which was carried before him, behind him a wall, in front the image of St Mary[3], all round him the memorials and relics of saints. Fitzurse rushed in, and asked some one in his way, "Where is the archbishop?" Before any one

---

[1] The monks.
[2] For this and the following details see the plan.
[3] No doubt standing over the altar of the Lady Chapel.

could answer, the archbishop replied, with a little movement of the head, "Here I am. Reginald, Reginald, I have
bestowed many benefits upon you. Do you come in to me
in arms?" "You shall see," he answered. "Are you that
traitor to the king? you shall come this way." And with
the point of his sword he struck off his cap. "I am no
traitor," he said. "I will not go out, you infamous man."
And he snatched the hem of his cloak[1] out of his hand.
Then Fitzurse roared, "Fly." "I will not fly," he rejoined; "you shall fulfil your evil purpose here." At these
words the murderer was taken aback, and sprang two or
three steps to the rear. He was about to strike, but hesi-
tated, either because he was gathering up his force, or
because the recollection of his lord's past behaviour made
him for the moment spare him. The other three meanwhile closed upon him, saying fiercely, "You shall die this
moment." "If you want my head," he said, "I command
you under pain of anathema not to hurt any of those
around us. I gladly accept death, if only the church by
my blood may obtain freedom and peace." He spoke, and
stretching his head forwards held it in position for the blow,
chanting his last words, "To God, and St Mary, and Denys
the martyr, and the patron saints of this church, I commend
my spirit and the cause of the church." Then Fitzurse,
eager for the glory of striking the first blow, and the advantage of losing his own soul quickly, bounded forward,
and with all his might inflicted a wound upon the outstretched head, and shouted, as if exulting over a conquered foe, "Strike, strike[2]!"

At this word, I who speak, thinking, like the rest, that

[1] Clearly not the archiepiscopal pall, which would be worn only
at mass.

[2] Dixit, caputque protensum ferientibus coaptavit, haec verba
novissima psallens, "Deo, et beatae Mariae, et martyri Dionysio,
patronisque hujus ecclesiae sanctis, commendo spiritum meum et
ecclesiae causam." Accelerans autem Ursides de primo ictu referre
tropaeum, et de festina perditione sua lucrum, prosiluit, et toto cona-
mine suo capiti protenso vulnus incussit, exclamavitque tanquam
devicto hoste triumphans, "Percutite, percutite."

I was going to be struck with the sword, being conscious of my sins, and far from fit for martyrdom, turned my back quickly and ran up the stairs, clapping my hands together. Thereupon, some who were still standing at prayer dispersed....So the murderers, set on by the author of confusion, heaped wounds upon the wound, and dashed out his brain[1].

A clerk, however, of English birth, named Edward, in loving anxiety for our father, held up his arm and caught one blow among the many; then, fearing more wounds and worse to follow, took refuge at the nearest altar, to which several of the brethren had already fled in fear of their lives, without knowing by whom he was struck. We can guess who was the author of the wound from the fact that William[2], when his accomplices were relating at Saltwood Castle what share each had borne in the savagery against the martyr, and were boasting of their crime, affirmed that he had cut off the arm of John of Salisbury. One of the brethren also received a blow while engaged in affectionate attendance upon our father. But the prayer of the good shepherd, after the example of the true Shepherd who said, "If ye seek Me, let these go their way," obtained that he alone should fall, without loss of any of the flock. So this monk was hit with the flat of the sword, and to his surprise carried his head away with him.

The knees of the martyr tottered; the house of clay was beginning to fall. While they were killing him, he prayed in silence; he sang with the understanding, he sang with the spirit also. As he fell, or actually lay prostrate, one of the murderers, not satisfied with what had been done, dashed the point of his sword on the stone floor; but the blade was shattered, and the Lord thus signified that the church triumphed in the blood of the martyr, and that wickedness was conquered....But iniquity was not even yet content. While the other four rushed away, a fifth repeated the

---

[1] In vulnere vulnera conferentes, cerebrum excusserunt.
[2] De Tracy.

crime, and assailing the corpse with the threats of an enemy drove the point of his sword into the empty skull[1].

## (2) William Fitzstephen.

### (*Materials*, Vol. III. p. 132.)

On the fifth day of Christmas, accordingly, the four barons of the king who have been mentioned, with all their men, and accompanied by the De Brock household from Saltwood, came to Canterbury. In addition to them, there were a number of soldiers, whom they had summoned by proclamation from the castles and the neighbourhood of Canterbury, as on the king's service. About twelve of these went softly to the archbishop's palace direct, with the four, while others went through the city to inform the magistrates and chief citizens and to give orders as on the king's behalf that all the citizens were to come with them, armed, to the archbishop's house, on the king's service. When the city showed surprise at their excitement, and refused their demands, they immediately ordered them to keep quiet, and not to stir, whatever they might see or hear. This was their object, either to get the help of the inhabitants of the city in their crime, or at any rate to prevent them from offering any hindrance or from interfering in behalf of their archbishop.

The advance party, consisting of the aforesaid barons and knights, were introduced into the inner apartment, where the archbishop was. It was about the tenth hour of the day. The archbishop had dined, but the servants of the household were still dining. As they entered, he greeted them: they did not reply to his greeting, or the reply was not heard. They sat down in front of him among the clerks and monks. Reginald Fitzurse began as follows: "Our lord the king over the water sends us to you, to absolve the bishops who were excommunicated on your arrival in England, to restore to office those who were sus-

---

[1] Vacuo vertice mucronem infixit.

pended, and then to go to his son the king, whom you wish
to uncrown, at Winchester, and make satisfaction for this
great enormity, and submit to the sentence of his court."
The archbishop answered, "It was not I who excommunicated those who were excommunicated, or suspended those
who were suspended, but our lord the pope, by his letters,
correcting in this manner his own sons, and punishing
those who had done wrong;—the archbishop of York,
because, when I was away and unbidden, and neither
knew nor gave my consent, he presumed, to the prejudice
of my church, to crown the young king—a right which
belonged to the church of Canterbury and to me—and that
in my own province, and in defiance of the letters of the
lord pope himself;—the bishops, because, being suffragans
of the church of Canterbury, who had professed obedience,
they permitted this action, and made no protest on behalf
of their mother church: It is not for me to revise the sentence of the lord pope; those whom he binds no lesser
authority can loose. But although in the archbishop's case
I have no power of loosing, nor of binding either, yet to my
suffragans of London and Salisbury I conceded, when I
was requested, that I would release them from the anathema, and would restore all the others who were suspended,
if only they would humbly ask for mercy, or would give
surety and stand an ecclesiastical judgment; but those who
met me refused. I am still prepared to act in that way.
The coronation of my lord the young king remains valid,
effective, and unchallenged; and the lord pope punishes the
wrong done by the man who crowned him without touching
the dignity of him who was crowned; because the dignity
of my office was usurped by an improper person, and in an
improper place, and for their silent acquiescence my
bishops are smitten. And all this had the permission of
my lord the king, and his licence given me on the day of
our reconciliation. Nor do I seek to disinherit the young
king; nay, I would wish him many kingdoms of the world,
if it could be done without injustice to their possessors.
The other day I had started to go to him—not to offer him

satisfaction, for I had never offended him, but to congratulate him on his advancement with all the respect due to my lord; but in London I met a message from him, bidding me go home. I am sorry for it." Thereupon they broke out immediately into unbridled threats. The archbishop said, "I wonder that you storm thus at me, and threaten me with harm. You know that my lord the king, on St Mary Magdalene's day, received me into his peace and favour; and I saw several of you present there, and, so far as I understood, you were pleased at it, and I returned to the country with the king's letters of safe conduct." Then Master John of Salisbury said to him, "My lord, speak more in private about that matter." "It is of no use," said the archbishop; "the things that they suggest and demand are such as I neither can nor ought to do." Reginald Fitzurse said, "From whom then do you hold your archbishopric?" He answered, "The spirituals from God and my lord the pope, the temporals and estates from my lord the king." Reginald said, "Do you not admit that you hold it all from the king?" "Certainly not," he said; "but we have to render to the king the things which are the king's, and to God the things that are God's." Reginald and the rest, as if he had said something outrageous, were furiously angry, and gnashed upon him with their teeth.

But the righteous Thomas was bold as a lion and felt no terror. For righteousness and the freedom of his church he was ready to strive to the death, for his soul's sake. And he said, "It is useless to threaten me. If all the swords in England were over my head, your terrors could not move me from keeping God's righteousness and from my duty to the lord pope. You shall find me foot to foot in the Lord's battle. Once I withdrew, like a frightened priest; but I have returned to my church in the counsel and obedience of my lord the pope. I shall never desert it again. If I am allowed to exercise my priesthood in peace, it is well with me; if not, God's will concerning me be done. Besides this, you know what there is between me and you; which makes me wonder the more that you dare to threaten the archbishop in his own house." This he said in reference to the fact that this Reginald, and William de Tracy, and Hugh de Morville, had made themselves his men, while he was chancellor, by personal act of fealty, saving their duty to the king. Each one of them on his knees had put himself under his authority and command. Infuriated by that which ought to have restrained them, and unable to contain themselves for anger, they cried, "There is nothing between us to the hurt of the king." Reginald said, "We dare indeed threaten the archbishop, and more than threaten. Let us go."

A great part of the archbishop's household was standing there, together with many clerks and some soldiers, who were drawn to the spot by hearing the loud voices. Looking at these, Reginald exclaimed, "We tell you on behalf of the king, whose men and loyal subjects you are, to go away from this man." Perhaps, like their comrades in the city, with regard to the citizens, so these men indoors were afraid that the household might make a struggle on behalf of their lord, and rise up against them. As all stood still without moving, Reginald promptly gave the opposite order, "We charge you to keep this man; do not let him get away." The archbishop answered, "I am easy to keep; I shall not get away." The ruffians saw among the rest a knight, William Fitznigel, who waited upon the archbishop at table, who for some reason had hastened to the spot from a chamber of his own. They laid hold on him and led him away, saying, "You shall come with us." The knight called to the archbishop, "My lord, do you see what they are doing with me?" He answered, "I see. This is their violence, and the power of darkness." And rising up, the archbishop followed them—they had not yet left the chamber—a few steps, asking them gently enough to let his knight go. They obstinately withdrew, and meeting another knight of the archbishop's, Ralph Morin, they took him likewise with them; and as they passed through the midst of the hall and the courtyard, to join their followers, they cast terrible looks and threats in all directions, shouting, "Men! to arms, to arms!"

Meanwhile the whole band of the enemy got together in a big house exactly opposite the archbishop's gate, belonging to a man called Gilbert. Hearing the word of command, they rushed forth at a bound, entered the archbishop's gate, which stood open to them and was immediately shut, and kept shouting fearful cries of "King's soldiers! King's men! King's men!" For some of their comrades, having sent the best known softly ahead, lest the gate should be shut at the noise, were inside the archbishop's gate: they had removed the archbishop's gatekeeper, and substituted one of their own, that no one from the city might come in to the rescue of the archbishop, and no one go out to carry any tidings of what was happening to him. In front of the closed gate, of which only the wicket was open, and inside the courtyard of the hall, stood among the horses that William Fitznigel who has been mentioned before, at table the archbishop's man and knight, now against him. The same duty was assigned also to Simon de Crioil, a knight of the abbot of St Augustine's who lived near. Reginald armed himself apart in the forehall itself, and forced a scullion of the archbishop, called Robert Tibia, to help and serve him. Reginald took an axe from a carpenter who was repairing some steps there.

We, meanwhile, who remained with the lord archbishop in the chamber, talked over their words and threats, and the answers of the archbishop. We were not all of the same mind. Some thought that there was nothing to fear; the men had come drunk; they would not have spoken like that before dinner. "It is Christmas," they said; "the king's peace is pledged to us." Others were afraid that they would carry their threats into action. Many signs of their murderous determination had been observed. Meanwhile, we heard from the direction of the church a piteous noise of people of both sexes and all ages, lamenting for us, as sheep of the slaughter. They had seen the men in the city, armed and hastening by order to the archbishop's. On this side, we heard our men running down the stairs to go to church, and flying through the middle of the hall from the face of the men at arms, who were entering the courtyard by the gate that was opened to them. Osbert and Algar, and some others in the service of the archbishop, seeing the men at arms rushing in, shut the hall door, and strengthened it with a bar. Robert de Brock, seeing this, began with a hatchet to destroy a certain partition, by which means he forced his way into the inner parts of the house, and opened the hall door to the assassins, grievously beating and wounding the men who had fastened the door. We clerks inside with the archbishop could hear the blows of Robert de Brock, as he broke through the wall. How could we, the monks, the clerks, and associates of the archbishop, help feeling fear and terror?....But the good Thomas despised death....

Then the monks, many of whom were there, said to him, "Go into the church, lord." He replied, "Nothing of the kind. Do not be afraid. Monks are generally too timid and cowardly." They did not acquiesce. Some laid hands on him and lifted him from his seat, and forced him. Others persuaded him that he ought to go because the monks were already saying evensong, and that he had meant to hear nones and evensong. Accordingly he ordered the Lord's cross to be carried forward. One of his clerks, Henry of Auxerre, bore it. When we got into the monks' cloister, the monks wished to bar the door behind him. Thomas was vexed and would not have it, and at a slow pace came last, putting all in front of him as the good shepherd puts his sheep. Fear, which the love of God had cast out, was as far from his outward bearing as from the inner fortress of his mind. Once indeed he cast a glance over his right shoulder; I do not know whether it was to see if the king's men were hard on his footsteps, or to see that no one was left behind to bolt the door.

He entered the church itself. The monks of the church, as much frightened as surprised by such a great disturbance, left their evensong unfinished, and ran out of the choir to meet the lord archbishop as he entered the church, re-joicing and thanking God that they saw him alive and could welcome him. They had heard that his head was already cut off. Some were weeping for joy or fear, some urging one course and some another, like Peter when he said to our Lord, "This be far from Thee"; but Thomas, who was not afraid to die for the freedom and cause of the church, told them to go away and leave him. He did not wish them to hinder his passion, the coming of which he had foretold, and now saw that it was at hand. He intended to go to the altar up above, where he usually heard private masses and the hours[1], and had already gone up four steps, when Reginald Fitzurse, in his coat of mail, and with his sword drawn, presented himself in advance of his associates at the cloister door by which we had come in, and shouted, "Now, king's men, after me!" In a moment he was joined by the other three, covered like him with coats of mail, body and head, all but their eyes, and with their swords bared. A number of others bearing arms, but without coats of mail, were with them, who belonged to their following and their company; and some also from the town of Canterbury, whom they had forced to come with them....When they saw the armed men, the monks wished to fasten the church door; but the good man, trusting in God, and not alarmed with sudden fear at the assault of the powers of the ungodly, turned back and came down the steps, forbidding them to shut the church door, and saying, "God forbid that we should make a castle of the church of God. Let all who wish to come into the church of God come in. God's will be done." Then, as he was going down the steps, John of Salisbury, and all his clerks, except Robert the canon, and William Fitzstephen, and Edward Grim, who had newly come to him, clutching at the hope of protection, and endeavouring to put themselves in safety, left him, and made their way, some to the altars, some to hiding places.

And indeed if the archbishop had chosen to slip aside

[1] See the topographical Note B, pp. 63 foll.

and deliver himself by means of flight, he could easily have done it, for time and place offered him the opportunity unsought. It was evening; the longest night of the year was coming on: the crypt was close by, and in it plenty of dark and secret corners. There was also another door close at hand, by which he might have gone up a winding staircase to the chambers and vaults of the upper church[1]. There perhaps he would not have been discovered, or something might have happened in the interval. But he would have nothing of the kind. He did not slip away; he made no supplication to the smiters; he uttered no murmur of complaint in the whole course of his agony.... The frenzied executioners, unexpectedly finding the door open, ran into the church....One of them said to the monks who stood by with the archbishop, "Do not stir." And indeed at first, when they saw the archbishop, the look of him so confounded and surprised the assassins that they fell back in awe. Then some one cried, "Where is the traitor?" The archbishop, possessing his soul in patience, took no notice of the word. Again some one cried, "Where is the archbishop?" He answered, "Here I am, no traitor, but a presbyter of God, and I wonder at your coming into a church of God in that array. What do you want?" One of the assassins said, "That you should die: you cannot live any longer." Then he said, "I accept death in the name of the Lord; and I commend my soul and the cause of the church to God and blessed Mary and the patron saints of this church. Far be it from me to fly because of your swords; but with God's authority I charge you not to touch any of my people." One of them had both a sword and a two-edged axe, in order to break through the church door with the axe, in case it were fastened against them. Now, keeping his sword, he put down the axe, which is still preserved there.

One of them smote the archbishop between the shoulders

---

[1] Perhaps by the *camerae* Fitzstephen means the chambers of the convent, rather than upper recesses of the church. There was access up the turret, across the chapterhouse, to the great dorter.

with the flat of his sword, saying, "Fly; you are a dead
man." He stood his ground firmly, and offering his neck[1]
continued to commend himself to God, and named again
and again the holy archbishops who were martyrs, St
Denys and St Alphege of Canterbury. Some of them,
saying, "You are a prisoner; you shall come along with us,"
laid hands on him and endeavoured to drag him out of the
church, and yet were afraid that the people would rescue
him out of their hands. Replying, "I will go nowhither: you
shall do here what you wish to do—what you have been
ordered to do," he resisted as well as he could. The monks
also held him back, and along with them Master Edward
Grim; who, seeing William de Tracy brandishing his sword
over the archbishop's head for the first stroke, put his
arm in the way and caught it. The same stroke which
wounded him severely in the arm wounded the archbishop
also on the bowed head[2]....

The blood trickled down from the archbishop's head.
He wiped it off with his arm, and on seeing it he thanked
God saying, "Into Thy hands, O Lord, I commend my
spirit." His head received a second blow, which brought
him down first on his knees and then on his face, with his
hands joined and outstretched to God, beside the altar
of St Benedict which stood there. Care, or grace, made him
fall in seemly fashion, covered with his cloak to the heels,
as if for worship or prayer. He fell on his right side; it was
to the right hand of God that he was going. As he lay
there, Richard le Breton struck him with such force, that
the sword broke on his head and on the church floor,
saying as he did so, "Take that for love of my lord William,
the king's brother[3]"....

---

[1] Cervicem praebens.                    [2] In capite inclinato.

[3] Datur in caput ejus ictus secundus, quo et ille in faciem concidit,
positus primo genibus, conjunctis et extensis ad Deum manibus, secus
aram quae ibi erat sancti Benedicti; et curam habuit, vel gratiam,
ut honeste caderet, pallio suo coopertus usque ad talos, quasi adora-
turus et oraturus. Super dextram cecidit, ad dextram Dei iturus.
Eum procumbentem Ricardus Brito percussit tanta vi ut et gladius

The holy archbishop received in all four strokes, all of them on the head; and the whole crown of the head was cut off[1]. It could then be seen how his members were at the service of the spirit. Neither in mind, nor by raising or flinching of his limbs, was he seen to struggle against death....One Hugh of Horsea, surnamed Mauclerk, planting his foot on the neck of the holy martyr as he lay drew out with his sword's point the blood and brain from the cavity of the severed crown[2]....

For a long while he lay there almost alone, forsaken by clerks and monks and all the rest, and not even a light was as yet brought, to set by his sacred corpse. Osbert, his chamberlain, with a pocket knife cut off a piece of his own shirt, to cover what was left of his half-severed head[3].

When it was ascertained that the murderers had departed, his clerks and the monks, the servants, and a great number of people from the town, gathered round the holy archbishop. The silence was broken, and in every direction they all burst into groans and lamentations, which they had previously suppressed for fear of the murderers. Far on into the night the weeping and wailing were prolonged. At last they made up their minds to lay the body of the lord archbishop on a bier and carry it through the midst of the choir and set it before the altar, the gaping skull covered with a clean linen cloth, and the cap, over that again, acting as a bandage[4]. The archbishop's sweetness and constancy were still visible in his countenance. There again much weeping took place. Brother Robert, priest and canon of the religious house of Merton, an honourable man, who had been his chaplain and inseparable companion

ad caput ejus et ad ecclesiae pavimentum frangeretur; et ait, "Hoc habeas pro amore domini mei Willelmi, fratris regis."

[1] Quattuor omnino habuit ictus sanctus archiepiscopus, omnes in capite; et corona capitis tota ei amputata est.

[2] A concavitate coronae amputatae cum mucrone cruorem et cerebrum extrahebat.

[3] Unde semiputati capitis ejus reliquum contegeret.

[4] Cranii vacuitate cooperta cum lineo mundo, pileolo desuper astringente.

from the day of his ordination, after commending the truly religious and honourable character of the lord archbishop, of which, as his confessor, he was qualified to speak, proceeded to show the monks, what none of us knew before, that the archbishop was in haircloth, and thrusting his hand into his bosom, showed the haircloth next to his skin; and over the haircloth a monk's habit....

After a little while, a monk of the church, Arnold the goldsmith, and some others with him, returned to the scene of the martyrdom; they collected his blood and brain, which had been poured out over the floor of the church, with great decency into a basin; and to prevent the spot from being trampled by passing feet, they placed some portable benches across it. The watch was kept that night in piety, sanctity, and soberness. The monks only said in silence the commendation of the departed soul.

The next day, a report was heard in the church that the household of De Brock with their accomplices had made preparations to drag him out of the church, being sorry that they had killed him there; and in fear of this the monks made haste to bury the sacred body and lay it in a tomb. There were present at the burial the abbot of Boxley and the prior of Dover, who had been previously summoned by the archbishop, because he desired their advice in making one of the monks prior, as there was not one in the church of Canterbury[1]. They came to the decision that he should have no other washing than the wash-

---

[1] The Dean of Wells has most kindly given me the following interesting note on these words of Fitzstephen.

*The Priory of Dover.*

The following Instruments are Dugdale (ed. 1823, IV. 538 f.):

Charter of Henry I granting St Martin's Church to Abp Wm. de Corboil for regular Canons.

Confirmation of this charter by Innocent II.

Charter of Henry II (attested by Thomas the Chancellor) granting the same to the church of Canterbury and Abp Theobald; and ordaining that the Monastic order according to the rule of St Benedict, introduced by authority of Innocent II and Abp Theobald, be for ever there maintained;

ing with his own blood; and removing and distributing his daily upper clothing they buried him in the hair-shirt in which they found him, and the breeches of linen lined

> and that none should have power of disposition of its affairs save the Archbishop of Canterbury.
>
> Letters Patent of Edw. III (1356) permitting Simon Islip arch-bishop to unite the priory of Dover with the priory of Christ Church, Canterbury, so that the latter prior should have possession and disposition thereof in perpetuity.

Innocent II was pope from 1130–1143, so that before 1143 Theobald must have introduced, or obtained leave to introduce, monks from Canterbury, as the Dover Chronicle records (Dugdale, IV. 586).

It would seem as though towards the end of his primacy Theobald granted a charter to the prior and convent of Christ Church to the effect that the prior of Dover should always be a monk of their house. So the French narrative (Dugdale, IV. 534), written c. 1320 in a suit of the archbishop for the recovery of the advowson. He had no leave from pope or king; and Abp Baldwin disowned the grant, and appointed a Dover monk, Osbern, as prior (*ibid.*).

This gives us the situation at the time of St Thomas's death. He himself had attested a charter of the king which said that the arch-bishop had sole disposition of the priory. Theobald had given away something of the rights of his successors without any confirmation of his act. But he had previously put in his own chaplain, Richard, in 1157.

When Richard himself became archbishop he made Warin the Cellarer of Christ Church prior of Dover in his place.

Boxley was a Cistercian Abbey, founded some 25 years before. The Cistercians had a high repute at this time, and they were notably ready to give advice.

The passage of Fitzstephen *seems* to mean that the abbot of Boxley and the prior of Dover had been previously summoned to Canterbury by the archbishop, because at their advice he intended to make the prior, who was not a member of the church of Canterbury, one of the monks of that house.

It looks as though the abbot of Boxley and the prior of Dover had originated the proposal.

But, tempting as this interpretation is, it is contradicted by the fact that, according to Gervase who was in a position to know, Richard was already a monk of Canterbury before his appointment as prior of Dover (Gerv., Rolls Series, II. 397).

"Prior Dovorensis successit, Ricardus nomine, qui ab ineunte aetate in ecclesia Cantuariensi monachicum gesserat habitum. Qui cum esset de Normannia natus, artium liberalium scholas egressus, in ecclesia Cantuariensi susceptus sub regulari disciplina satis modeste simul et honeste conversatus est. Processu temporis Theodbaldi

with haircloth, and the same shoes on his feet, and the
monk's habit which he had on; and over these the vesture
that he had been ordained in—the alb, called in Greek
*poderes*—the plain amice, a chrisom cloth, a mitre, stole,
and maniple—all which he had ordered to be kept for him,
perhaps against the day of his burial. Over these he had,
as an archbishop, tunicle, dalmatic, chasuble, pall and pins,
chalice, gloves, ring, buskins, pastoral staff. Such is the
usual state, and he deserved it....

When everything belonging to the burial had been
arranged and settled, the sacred body of the archbishop,
amidst the grief and lamentation of many, was laid in a
new marble tomb—without mass, because the church had
been desecrated by the entrance of armed men—before two
altars in the crypt.

## (3) BENEDICT[1].

### (*Materials*, Vol. II. p. 1.)

On the fifth day of Christmas, as the archbishop was
sitting in his chamber about the eleventh hour of the day,

archiepiscopi capellanus effectus est; una cum beato Thoma eidem
sedulo ministravit... "

This is decisive unless the authority of Gervase is to be set aside.

We are thrown back therefore on an enquiry into the career of *Odo*.
He had been subprior [of Canterbury], and seems to have become
prior c. 1167, but not by the archbishop's appointment (*sine martyris
dispositione, Mater.* I. 542). He had not supported Thomas in his
exile, and had retired from Canterbury in 1169 [see *Dict. Nat. Biogr.*
"Odo of Canterbury"]. If the facts be as thus represented, it is
probable that Thomas did not recognise Odo as prior. He might well
wish for the counsel and support of two of the most respected religious
of his diocese, if he were about to set aside the prior who had presumably been elected by the monks and to choose a new monk to fill
his place.

His death prevented this purpose. Odo returned, converted like
the rest of the monks to admiration for the primate whom they had
failed to appreciate in his years of distress, and he retained his post
until he became abbot of Battle.

[1] The narrative of Benedict no longer exists in complete and separate form, but in fragments woven into the *Quadrilogus*, or Har-
mony of four Lives. In some cases the attribution there to Benedict
is incorrect; in some it is questionable.

and some clerks and monks sat round him, discussing
business plans with the archbishop, the four officers....en-
tered the archbishop's chamber. They received the usual
salutation from some who sat near the entrance, and returned the same, but in a low voice, and then advanced
to the archbishop. They seated themselves on the floor
before his feet, without saluting him either in their own
name or in the king's....When they had spent a little while
in this silence, to the perplexity of those who sat with them,
Reginald Fitzurse...addressed the saint as follows: "We
have been despatched to you by our lord the king across
the sea, and bring you his royal commands. We wish
therefore to know whether you would rather that we spoke
in secret or in public." The man of God...answered, "I
leave it to your choice and pleasure." "Then let it be in
secret," said Reginald, "and let these present withdraw for
a time." The saint...bade his men leave the room. When
they were gone out, and only the four officers were left in
the chamber with the archbishop, the doorkeeper ran up
and set the door open, that those who had now seated
themselves outside...might be able to keep an eye both
on their lord and on those enemies of God. When Reginald
had declared certain commands of the king, and the prudent man of God observed that they offered no likelihood
of peace or any good, remembering also the words of the
gospel, which seemed to him like a prophecy of what was
coming, "Jesus did not commit Himself unto them, because
He knew all men," he called the doorkeeper, and gave orders
that his clerks and the monks also who were there should
draw near, but all lay people be kept out.

[A lengthy account of the interview follows, which
concludes thus:]

"Since I find no right and no justice on either side, I will
exercise such justice as an archbishop can and ought, and
will not part with it for any mortal man." At this expression, one of them cried out, "Threats, threats! will
you put the whole land under an interdict, and excommunicate us all?" and another, "So help me God, he shall

not do it; he has put too many under the ban." Then they sprang up, and gave free vent to their passion and their revilings, swinging their gauntlets round, waving their arms furiously, and displaying their frenzy alike by gesture and by violent noise. The archbishop also arose. In the great uproar and the confusion of voices it was not easy to make out what words of venom were uttered by which of the men against the Lord's anointed. At last the sons of Belial turned to the monks who were there, and attempted—in vain, it must be acknowledged—to arm them against their own father and the father of the whole country by saying, "On behalf of our lord the king, we charge you to keep this man carefully, that he may not get away, and to deliver him over to the king at the king's pleasure." This speech they repeated again and again; but the kind father answered for his sons, "What do you mean? Do you think that I wish to flee away and escape? I will not flee, either for the king or for any man alive. I did not come to flee, but to abide the rage of ruffians, and the malice of the wicked." "True, true," the officers said; "please God, you shall not escape...."

As they left the room with great uproar and insulting words, and with many threats, the archbishop accompanied them to the door of the chamber, calling upon Hugh de Morville, who was superior to the rest by birth and ought to have been so in character, to come back and talk to him. But on his departure, with the rest, in pride and scorn, for they could no longer contain themselves for anger the man of God came back and sat down again, and complained before his people of these commands of the king and of the outrageous language of the officers. But one of his clerks—it was the learned Master John of Salisbury, a man of great eloquence and profound wisdom, and, what is yet more, deeply rooted in the fear and love of God—said in answer to these complaints, "Lord, it is very strange that you do not take the advice of anybody. What need was there for a man of such eminence to stand up, and so only excite those men's ill will the more, and to go after them to the door? Would it not have been better to take counsel with those present and to give them a gentler answer? They are devising against you every mischief that they can, that if nothing else, they may provoke you to anger and catch you in your words." The saint...said, "My plan is now completed. I know well enough what I ought to do." Master John answered, "I hope to God that it may turn out well."

The profane knights, on going out, hastened to their comrades and accomplices in the court, and arming themselves quickly, returned in coats of mail, with swords and hatchets, bows and arrows, two-edged axes and other implements, either for breaking through bars and doors, or for effecting the crime which they intended. Certain persons, however, ran before to the archbishop and cried, "Lord, lord, they are arming." He answered, "What do I care? Let them arm."

There was in their detestable company that son of perdition, Robert de Brock, whom we have mentioned as having been excommunicated and put under anathema by the saint on Christmas Day because of his monstrous misdeeds. This man knew all the ins and outs of the palace, because during the archbishop's banishment he had had charge of the whole archbishopric under his lord, Ranulf de Brock. When they were preparing to seize the door of the hall, the servants prudently shut them out. Finding that the door was shut and barred, so that entrance was denied them, they turned forthwith under the guidance of this Robert to some less frequented stairs, which led down from the outer chamber into the orchard, and, breaking through the nearest window, they got the door[1] also unfastened.

When the servants ran ahead to the brave champion of God and clamoured at him on every side to flee, he, thinking nothing of death for Christ, neither moved from the place, nor was shaken in mind....But the few monks who happened to be there broke the bolt of the door leading

[1] That of the great hall.

through the cloister to the church, and strove to get their father away, in spite of his unwillingness, suggesting to him as an honourable reason for going that it was the hour for him to perform the service of evensong in the church. Others laid hands on him and lifted him from his seat, and forced him. Then the saint, remembering to fulfil even to the letter the Lord's precept, "Whosoever will come after Me, let him deny himself, and take up his cross, and follow Me," ordered his cross to be carried before him. When he came out, those who accompanied him pressed him to go faster, but he stopped short, ashamed to seem to flee. The monks persisted, and urged him vehemently to go on. Either because they were behaving less respectfully than usual, or to strengthen and comfort those about him, he repeated again and again the question, "What is all this, sirs? what are you afraid of?" When they got to the cloister door, and could not force it open, and had no keys to hand, two cellarers of the church of Canterbury, Richard and William, who had heard the uproar and the clash of arms, hastened to the spot by way of the cloister, tore away the bolt, and opened the door to the approaching archbishop....

Some of the monks left evensong and ran to meet him; and bringing their pastor in, though he resisted, they began to shut the church doors to keep the enemy out. But the holy father turning back at once rebuked them, saying, "Let my people come in"; and going to the door he threw it open, and removing both sets of people[1] from the doorway, he began with his own sacred hands to pull into the church his men who had been left outside to the teeth of the wolves, saying as he did so, "Come in, come in, faster."
...At last the urgency of his own sons dragged him violently away, and he left the open doors; but the enemy were by that time close to them....

The man of God could well have slipped away from that hour of death, if he had been so minded, when the officers

[1] Apparently those who joined him from the choir, and those who had come with him through the cloister.

were entering the minster, some crying, "Where is the traitor?" others, "Where is the archbishop?" But the saint, knowing in the spirit all things that should come upon him, came down from the flight of stairs, of which he had mounted a few, to meet them, saying with a calm countenance, "Here I am; no traitor, but the archbishop."... The first of them stepped up and said to the saint, "Flee; you are a dead man." The saint answered, "I shall certainly not flee." Then the sacrilegious officer laid his hand on him, and knocking off his cap with the edge of his sword, said, "Come this way; you are a prisoner." "I will not come," said the saint, "you shall do here what you wish to do to me," and he snatched the hem of his cloak out of his hand....

To another man in mail, whom he saw coming on with bared sword, he turned and said, "What is this, Reginald? I have bestowed many benefits upon you, and do you come to me in church in arms?"...The officer, full of the spirit of frenzy, answered, "You shall know in a moment; you are a dead man."...

With bowed head he awaited the coming of a second stroke. When the second stroke descended on his head, he fell to the ground with his body straight out, as if prostrate in prayer. A third man cut off the greater part of his head, horribly enlarging the former wound. A fourth, on being chidden by one of them for hanging back from striking, dashed his sword with great force into the same wound, and breaking the sword on the marble pavement, left both the point and the hilt to the church[1]....What could the breaking of the sword of the adversaries be taken to signify, but the real overthrow of the power of the enemy, and the victory

---

[1] Inclinato capite secundi vulneris praestolabatur adventum. Secundo vero vulnere capiti ejus inflicto, recto corpore quasi ad orationem prostratus in terram corruit. Tertius autem plurimam testae portionem amputando vulnus praecedens horribiliter ampliavit. Quartus autem, ab uno eorum quod ferire tardaret correptus, in idem vulnus vi magna gladium vibravit, gladioque in pavimento marmoreo confracto tam cuspidem quam gladii sui capulum reliquit ecclesiae.

of the church through the martyr's blood? Nor was the child of Satan satisfied with committing such an atrocity upon God's priest. Horrible as it is to relate, he drove his sword into the sacred head of the dead man, cast out the brain, and scattered it savagely on the pavement, calling to his partners in the crime, "He is dead; let us get away at once." From this it may be gathered that they were afraid lest some of the knights or servants of the holy martyr might come upon them and avenge their lord's blood. As they went out of the minster they shouted, "King's knights! king's men!" as if in battle, in token of their splendid victory. Others said mocking, "He wished to be king; he wished to be more than king. Let him be king now! Let him be king now!"...

When the sacred body was lifted from the ground,... there were found under it an iron hammer and a two-headed axe which the murderers had left....His head was surrounded with a kind of diadem of blood[1], as if in token of his sanctity, but the face was entirely free from blood, except for one slight streak that had run down from the right side of the forehead to the left side of the face across the bridge of the nose[2]. While he still lay on the pavement, some smeared their eyes with his blood, others brought vessels with them and pilfered what part they could, others vied with each other in dipping strips off their garments in it; and no one afterwards thought himself fortunate who had not carried home at any rate some little portion of the precious treasure. And indeed in that agitated scene of confusion any one could do what he liked. But part of the blood which they left to the church was gathered with great decency into a suitable vessel and placed in the church to be kept. His cloak and his outer frock, all stained as they were with blood, were given away to the poor for the benefit of his soul. This was an indiscreet act of charity; the recipients would have been much to be envied, if they

---

[1] Cum cruor ad instar diadematis...capiti circumfusus jacuisset.

[2] A dextra frontis parte in faciem sinistram per transversum nasi descenderat.

had not thoughtlessly sold the articles forthwith, caring less for them than for the small sum that they fetched....

The next day,...the monks, alarmed both for themselves and for the saint, lest the saint should be treated ignominiously and themselves lose their precious treasure, set to work to bury him with the utmost haste. On this account they were unable either to wash his sacred corpse, or, according to the custom of the holy church of Canterbury, to rub it with balm....But when they took off his outer garments to vest him in pontificals, they found that the body was clothed in haircloth, of which the hardness itself was a torture, not to speak of other reasons, and, what we never read or heard of as done by any saint, that his under-breeches also were of haircloth down to the knees, and that over these he wore a monk's habit, that is, a smock and a hood. They gazed at one another, in astonishment at the sight of this concealed and incredible religion.

### (4) JOHN OF SALISBURY.

*(Materials,* Vol. II. p. 319.)

Being to suffer, in the church,...before the altar, the martyr of Christ, before he was smitten, heard himself sought by the knights who had come for the purpose, as they shouted in the midst of the crowd of bystanders, "Where is the archbishop?" He went to meet them from the stairs which he had partly mounted, saying with a calm countenance, "Here I am; what do you want?" to which one of the murderous knights answered in a spirit of frenzy, "That you should die at once; you cannot live any longer." The archbishop answered with as great firmness of speech as of mind..."And I am ready to die for my God and for the assertion of righteousness and the liberty of the church. But if you seek my head, I forbid you, on behalf of God almighty, and under pain of anathema, to hurt any other in any wise, whether monk or clerk or layman, greater or less; but let all stand clear of the punishment as they stand clear of the cause. It is not to be laid to their charge, but to mine, if any of them have espoused the cause of the suffering church. I willingly embrace death, if only the church by my blood may obtain peace and liberty."...

When he had said this, seeing the slaughterers with their drawn swords, he bowed his head like a man in prayer[1], uttering these last words, "To God and blessed Mary, and the patron saints of this church, and blessed Denys, I commend myself and the cause of the church."

Who can relate what followed without sighs and sobs and tears? Pity does not allow me to tell in detail what the ruthless slaughterers...did. It did not satisfy them to profane the church and pollute the sacred day with the blood and death of the priest; they must needs cut off the crown of his head, which had been consecrated to God by the anointing of the holy chrism, and then, horrible as it is to tell, with their murderous swords they cast out the dead man's brain and scattered it savagely over the pavement with blood and bones[2]....But in all these sufferings... the martyr did not utter a word or a cry, nor give a groan, nor hold up an arm or a garment against the smiter, but held his head, which he had presented bowed to the swords, unflinching till all was finished. Then falling to the ground with his body straight out, he moved neither hand nor foot, while the assassins boasted that by the traitor's death they had restored peace to the country....

The frenzy of the persecutors was not appeased with all this. They said that the traitor's body must not be buried among the holy bishops, but cast into a filthy slough, or hung on a gibbet. So the holy men who were there, fearing that violence would be applied to them, buried him in the crypt, before the servants of Satan, who had been summoned for the sacrilege, could assemble, before the altar

[1] In modum orantis inclinavit caput.

[2] Nisi corona capitis, quam sacri chrismatis unctio Deo dicaverat, amputata,...funestis gladiis jam defuncti ejicerent cerebrum et per pavimentum cum cruore et ossibus crudelissime spargerent.

of St John the Baptist and St Augustine the apostle of England, in a marble sarcophagus.

## (5) EDWARD GRIM.

*(Materials, Vol. ii. p. 430.)*

The hour of the repast was over, and the saint had just withdrawn from the multitude with those of his household into the inner part of the house, to attend to business. The multitude waited outside in the yard, while the four went in alone, with a single attendant. They were met with honour, as servants of the king, and well known persons, and were invited to the table. Those who waited on the archbishop were still eating. They refused food; they were thirsting for blood. At their bidding, the archbishop was informed that four men were come, who desired to speak with him on the king's behalf. He assented, and they were ushered in, but for a long time they sat in silence, neither saluting the holy archbishop, nor addressing him. Nor did the judicious man himself salute them immediately upon their entrance, in order to ascertain their inward intention by the question which they should put, according to the meaning of the text, "By thy words thou shalt be justified." But after some delay he turned towards them, and carefully scanning each of their countenances he saluted them peaceably. The unhappy men, who had made a covenant with death, answered his salutation with curses, and ironically prayed God to help him. At this word of bitterness and malice the man of God blushed an extraordinary colour knowing well that the men had come on purpose to hurt him.

The one who appeared to take the lead, and to be the readiest for crime, Fitzurse, breathing fury, burst into these words: "We have certain things to say to you by the command of the king. If you wish us to rehearse them before a number of people, say so." Knowing what they had to say, and where it came from, the archbishop answered, "These things ought not to be produced in a private chamber, but in public." But the miscreants were so bent upon the death of the archbishop, that if the door-keeper had not recalled the clerks (for the archbishop had ordered them all out), they would have transfixed him, as they afterwards confessed, with the shaft of the cross which stood beside him. On the return of those who had gone out, the person above mentioned began his false indictment of the man of God in these words. "The king, after making peace with you, sent you back to your own see, as you asked, putting an end to all quarrels; but you, on the contrary, adding insult to your former injuries, have broken the compact of peace, and have dealt proudly against your lord to your own hurt. Those who crowned the king's son, and exalted him to the dignity of the kingship, you in your stubborn haughtiness have sentenced to suspension; the king's ministers, by whose prudent counsels the affairs of the realm are carried on, you have excommunicated; thus showing that, if you could, you would deprive the king's son of his crown. Your intrigues, and your determination to accomplish your devices against your lord, are notorious. If therefore you are disposed to come and answer for these things in the presence of the king, say so. This is what we were sent for." The archbishop answered him, "It was never my wish, I call God to witness, to deprive my lord the king's son of his crown or to diminish his power. I would rather wish him three crowns, and would help him in reason and equity to conquer the most ample kingdoms of the earth. It is unreasonable that my lord the king should be angry, if, as you object, my own men in the various cities and towns meet me and accompany me. For seven years my exile has robbed them of the comfort which my presence would have given. And at this moment I am ready to give satisfaction, if I have done anything wrong, in any place that my lord likes; but he has forbidden me with threats to enter his cities, towns, or even villages. Besides, it was not I, but my lord the pope, who suspended the prelates from their office." "It was through you," cried the infuriated man, "that they were suspended, and you must absolve them." "I do not deny," he answered, "that it was done through me; but the thing is above me; it is not for one of my degree to absolve those whom the lord pope has bound. Let them go to him. Their contempt for me and for their mother the church of Christ of Canterbury affects him."

"Now then," said the slaughterers, "this is the king's commandment, that you leave the realm and his dominions with all that belong to you; for there will be no peace for you or any of yours from this day onward, because you have broken the peace." He replied, "An end to your threats, and stop your wrangling. I trust in the King of heaven who suffered for His people on the cross; for no man henceforth shall see the sea between me and my church. I did not come to run away; any one who wants me will find me here. But it would not beseem my lord the king to send me such a message; the outrage offered to me and mine by the king's ministers would have been enough, without threatening me for the future." "This," they answered, "was the king's message, and we will prove it; for when you ought to have respected the king's majesty and to have referred the redress of your wrongs to his judgment, you followed your angry self will, and cast the king's ministers and servants out of the church with disgrace." The champion of Christ, lifting himself up against his accusers in the fervour of the Spirit, answered them, "Whosoever shall presume to violate the constitutions of the holy see of Rome and the rights of the church of Christ, and will not come of his own accord to make reparation, I will not spare him, whosoever he may be, nor will I delay to punish the offender with the censure of the church." This saying made the knights start forwards, unable to bear the firmness of the answer. "We declare to you," they said, "that you have spoken at the peril of your head." "Have you come to kill me?" he asked. "I have committed my cause to the Judge of all men. Threats do not move me, nor are your swords more ready to strike than my soul

is for martyrdom. Look for some one else to run away:
you shall find me foot to foot in the battle of the Lord."
As they went out with noise and insults, the one whom
we have rightly called the Bear cried out brutally, "On
the king's behalf we charge you, both clerks and monks,
to take this man into custody and keep him safe, that he
may not slip away and escape, until the king has taken full
justice of his person." So saying they departed, and the
man of God accompanied them to the door, himself crying
out, "You shall find me here, here," and placing his hand
upon the back of his neck, as if showing the spot where
they were about to smite him.

When he had returned to the place where he was sitting
before, he comforted his own people in the Lord, and ex-
horted them not to be afraid; and as it seemed to us who
were there, he sat down again as calmly—he whom alone
they sought to kill—as if they had come to invite him to a
wedding. A few minutes after, the slaughterers came back
in coats of mail, with swords, and hatchets, and axes, and
all sorts of tools handy for the crime that they intended.
Finding the house doors bolted, and that their knocking
got no opening, they took a less frequented way through
the orchard, which brought them to a wooden obstacle,
which they hacked and hewed and destroyed. At the
terrible noise of violence, nearly all the servants and clerks,
like sheep before the wolves, were scattered in terror to
right and left. Those who remained cried out to him to
flee to the church; but he, remembering his assurance
that no fear of death should make him run away from the
slayers, refused to flee....The monks insisted, saying that
he ought not to be absent from evensong, which was just
being said in the church. He stayed motionless in the place
of less reverence,...lest, as has been said, reverence for the
sacred building should baulk the ungodly of their purpose,
and deprive the saint himself of his heart's desire. So sure
was he of being removed by martyrdom from this life of
misery, that after his return from exile, he is reported to
have said in the hearing of many, "You have here the

martyr Alphege, a true saint, and beloved of God: God's mercy will provide you with another; He will not tarry. "... But when neither argument nor entreaty could induce him to take refuge in the church, the monks, in spite of his refusal and resistance, seized him, dragged, carried, and pushed him; and paying no heed to his reproachful efforts to make them let him go, they brought him at last into the church. The door through which a way led into the monks' cloister had for many days been carefully barred, and when the tormentors were close upon their heels, this door took away all confidence of escape; but one of them ran forward, and at the first touch, to the astonishment of all, he got the bar out as easily as if it had been stuck with glue.

As soon, however, as the monks had got inside the church door, the four knights came running after them as fast as they could. With them was a subdeacon, armed with the same malice as the knights, named Hugh Mauclerk—a name which his iniquity deserved, for he had no respect for God nor for the saints, as his subsequent conduct proved. As the holy archbishop entered the minster, the monks, who had begun evensong, left the service and ran and met him, glorifying God that they saw their father alive and safe, when they had heard that he was killed. They hastened to bolt the doors of the church, to keep the enemy from slaying their pastor. But that wonderful champion turned to them and ordered the doors to be opened. "It will not do," he said, "to make the house of prayer, the church of Christ, into a fortress. Even when not shut, it is defence enough for those who belong to it. We shall triumph over the enemy by suffering rather than by fighting. We did not come to fight, but to suffer." Immediately the sacrilegious men stepped into the house of peace and reconciliation with swords drawn, striking no small terror into the beholders even by their looks and the clash of their arms. Amidst the confusion and hubbub of the people present—for those who had been attending evensong had run to the scene of the tragedy—the knights cried out in fury, "Where is Thomas Becket, traitor to the king and the kingdom?" He made no answer, and they shouted more vehemently, "Where is the archbishop?" At that word, quite undismayed, according as it is written, "The righteous shall be bold as a lion," he came down to meet them from the step to which the monks had carried him for fear of the soldiers, and in a voice that could be well heard, answered, "Here I am, no traitor to the king, but a priest. Why do you look for me?" And as he had said before that he was not afraid of them, he added, "Look, I am ready to suffer in the name of Him who redeemed me with His blood. God forbid that I should flee because of your swords, or go back from righteousness." Having said thus, he turned to the right, under a pillar, having on one side the altar of the blessed Mother of God, the ever-virgin Mary, and on the other that of St Benedict the confessor.... The slaughterers pressed upon him, saying, "Absolve and restore to communion those whom you have excommunicated, and give back their office to those who are suspended." "They have made no reparation," he said, "and I will not absolve them." "And you," they cried, "shall die, as you deserve." "And I," he answered, "am prepared to die for my Lord that by my blood the church may gain liberty and peace; but in the name of God almighty I forbid you to do any harm to my men, whether clerk or layman."...

Then they set upon him, and laid their sacrilegious hands upon him, grappling with him and dragging him, to get him outside the church and either kill him there, or bind him and carry him away, as they afterwards confessed. But it was not easy to move him from the pillar; and when one of them pressed hard upon him and came very close, he thrust him away, calling him a bawd, and saying, "You must not touch me, Reginald; you owe me fealty and obedience; you and your accomplices are behaving like fools." Enraged at being pushed back, the knight burst into fury, and brandishing his sword over the sacred head, he cried, "I owe you no fealty and no obedience contrary to my fealty to my lord the king." So the unconquerable martyr, perceiving that the hour was at hand that should put an end to mortal misery, and that the crown of immortality prepared for him and promised by the Lord was very nigh, bowed his head as for prayer, and joining his hands together and lifting them up aloft[1] commended his cause and that of the church to God, and St Mary, and the blessed martyr Denys.

He had scarcely uttered the words, when the wicked knight, fearing that he would be rescued by the people and escape alive, sprang suddenly at him, and wounded him— the lamb that was to be sacrificed to God—in the head. The blow shore off the top of his crown, which had been consecrated to God by the anointing of the holy chrism; and by the same blow the forearm of the narrator was cut[2]. For when all alike, monks and clerks, ran away, the narrator clave steadfastly to the holy archbishop, clasping him in his arms and holding him fast, until the arm that he held up was cut....Then the martyr received another blow on the head, but still remained motionless. A third stroke made him bend his knees and his elbows, offering himself as a living sacrifice, and saying in a low voice, "For the name of Jesus and in defence of the church I am ready to welcome death." As he lay thus, a third knight struck a heavy blow, by which the sword was dashed on the stone, and the crown, which was large, was so severed from the head, that the blood[3], whitened with the brain, and the brain, reddened with the blood, brought the colours of the lily and the rose to the face of the virgin mother church by the life and death of the confessor and the martyr. The fourth knight kept off those who approached, that the

[1] Inclinata in modum orantis cervice, junctis pariter et elevatis sursum manibus.

[2] Insiliit in eum subito, et summitate coronae, quam sancti chrismatis unctio dicaverat Deo, abrasa, agnum Deo immolandum vulneravit in capite, eodem ictu praeciso brachio haec referentis.

[3] Quo ictu et gladium collisit lapidi, et coronam, quae ampla fuit, ita a capite separavit ut sanguis, etc.

rest might accomplish the murder with greater freedom and ease. The fifth—not a knight, but that clerk who came in with the knights—that the martyr, who had been like Christ in other things, might have, like Him, a fifth wound, put his foot on the neck of the holy priest and precious martyr, and, horrible as it is to relate, scattered brain and blood on the pavement, crying to the rest, "Let us be off, knights; the man will not get up again."

In all this the illustrious martyr displayed the virtue of an extraordinary steadfastness, neither lifting, as might be expected of human weakness, hand or garment to protect himself from the smiter, nor uttering a word when smitten, nor letting a cry or groan or any sound of pain escape him, but holding the head which he had bowed motionless to the bare swords, until covered with blood and brain he laid his body on the pavement as if prostrate in prayer, and placed his spirit in Abraham's bosom....

The next day, while the sacred body was still kept in the church awaiting burial, one of the king's officers came at an early hour, and with sacrilegious persistence said, "This traitor perished rightly; it was an excellent and praiseworthy deed to get rid of him; he was endeavouring to take the crown away from the king's son." Then turning to the monks, he said, "Take the man away, and bury him as quickly as you can, and leave no trace of him, that his memory may perish from the earth, because of what he did against the king his lord. Otherwise I will have him torn in pieces with horses, and throw him into a stinking pit, for swine and dogs to devour." Anxious and frightened at this,...they made hasty preparations to bury him in the crypt. But first, on stripping the martyr's pure corpse for the customary washing, they found that beneath the habit of a canon regular he wore that of a monk and had been long in secret a member of that order, without even his intimate friends knowing it. Below this again, they found a hair-shirt next his skin,...and, what we never heard of any saint doing before, he had used tight breeches of hair-cloth....The sight touched the monks with a sense of his wonderful and unsuspected religion, and they cried, "Look, look! he is indeed a monk, and we never knew him."...

Having buried the venerable body in the crypt with fitting honour and reverence, they placed the sacred blood, which they had taken off the pavement, together with the brain, outside the tomb. It was an inspiration from on high that taught them not to enclose these with the body; for the healing draught soon brought so many benefits, that if they should be written every one, it would be too much for the faith of the weak.

## (6) Garnier de Pont St Maxence.

(Ed. Hippeau[1].)

(p. 191) The family of Satan came to the minster. Each one held in his right hand his naked sword, in the other the hatchets and the fourth a two-edged axe. A pillar was there, to support the vault, which hid the holy archbishop from them. Three of them went one side of the pillar: they sought and asked for "the traitor to the king." Reginald on the other side encountered a monk, and asked for the archbishop. Then the saint spoke: "Reginald, if thou seekest me," he said, "thou hast found me here." The name of traitor St Thomas heard not, but at the name of

La meisnie al Sathan est el muster venue;
En sa destre main tint chascuns s'espée nue;
En l'autre les cuingnies et li quarz besagüe.
Un piler ot iluec, la volte ad sostenue,
Ki del saint arcevesque lur toli la veüe;
    D'une part del piler en sunt li trei alé:
"—Le traïtur le Rei" unt quis et demandé.
Renalz, de l'autre part, un moine a encuntré;
Demanda l'arcevesque. Dunc a li sainz parlé:
"Renalz, se tu me quiers, fet-il, ci m'as trové."
    Le nun de traïtur saint Thomas n'entendi;
Mès al nun d'arcevesque restut et atendi,

---

[1] I have given as footnotes the various readings of the edition of H. Bekker, 1844.

archbishop he stopped and heeded, and came down from the step to meet Reginald: "Reginald, if thou seekest me," he said, "here hast thou found me." By the edge of his mantle Reginald had seized him. "Reginald, so many benefits have I done thee," said the good priest, "and what seekest thou, of me in holy church in arms?" Reginald Fitzurse said, "Verily thou shalt know!" (He had dragged him to him, that was all changed.) "You are a traitor to the king," he said; "you shall come this way." For he sought to hale him out of the holy minster: I trow well that St Thomas at this deed was wroth, that thus Reginald pressed and pushed him. At Reginald's touch he drew himself back, and wrenched the edge of his mantle out of his hands. "Fly, evil man, from hence," said the holy priest. "I am no traitor, and ought not to be accused of it." "Fly," said Reginald, when he perceived it. "I will not do it," said the saint; "here you shall find me, and here shall you work your great felonies."

E encuntre Renalt del degré descendi:
"Renalz, se tu me quiers, trové, fet-il, m'as ci."
Par le corn[1] del mantel l'aveit Renalz saisi;
"Renalz, tanz biens t'ai fez, fet li buens ordenez,
"E que quiers-tu sur mei en sainte Eglise armez?"
Fet Renalz li fils Urs: "Certes vus le saurez!"
(Sachei l'aveit a sei, que tut fu remuez;)
"Traïtur le Rei estes, fet-il, chà en vendrez!"
    Kar hors del saint mustier traïner le quida;
Bien crei que saint Thomas à cele feiz s'ira
De ço que cil Renalz le detrest et buta[2].
Si ad enpeint Renalt k'arrère rehusa,
E la corn del mantel hors des mains li sacha.
    "Fui, malveis hum d'ici, fet li sainz ordenez[3].
"Jo ne sui pas traïtres, n'en dei estre retez!"
"—Fuiez," fet li Renalz, quant se fu purpensez.
"—Ne l'ferai, dit li sainz, ici me troverez,
"E voz granz felunies[4] ici acomplirez."

----

    [1] col, B.                    [2] sacha, B.
    [3] corunez, B.                [4] malveistiez, B.

Towards the north wing the brave man went, and held himself close up against a pillar. Between two altars was this pillar arranged; to the Mother of God was the lower one consecrated; the other was dedicated in the name of St Benedict. There the infuriated officers dragged and pulled him. "Absolve," they said, "those who are excommunicated, and those who by you are suspended and bound." "I will not do it," he said, "any more than I began it." Then together they threatened to kill him. He said, "I am not frightened of your threats. I am quite ready to suffer martyrdom, but let my men go; touch them not, and do to me only what you have to do." The good shepherd did not forget his sheep in death....

(p. 193, l. 6) Then the sons of the fiend seized him by the wrists, and began to drag and hale him violently, and would have laid him as a load on the neck of William; for they wished to kill or bind him there, outside. But from the pillar they could not take him away nor remove him....

> Devers l'ele del Nort s'en est li bers alez,
> E à un piler s'est tenuz et acostez.
> Entre dous altels ert cil pilers mesurez;
> A la mère Deu est cil de desuz sacrez;
> El non seint Beneit est li autres ordenez.
>
> Là l'unt tret et mené li ministre enragié:
> "Assolez, funt-il, cels qui sunt escummingié,
> "E cels ki sunt par vus suspendu et lacié!"
> "—N'en ferai, fet-il, plus que je n'ai commencié."
> A ocire l'unt dunc ensemble manacié.
>
> Fet-il: "De vos manaces ne sui espoantez;
> "Del martire suffrir sui del tut aprestez,
> "Mès les miens en leissiez aler, n'es adesez;
> "E fètes de mei sul ço que fère devez."
> N'a les suens li buens pastre[1] à la mort obliez....
>
> Dunc l'unt saisi as puinz li fil à l'aversier,
> Si l'commencent forment à trère et à sachier,
> E sur le col Willams le voldrent enchargier;
> Kar là hors le voleient ou occire ou lier.
> Mès del piler ne l'porent oster, ne esluingnier....

[1] prestres, B.

(l. 21) Nor would God that he should be vilely used. He did it to prove this evil people, whether they would dare to outrage the minster so cruelly. For there is none so felon, not even in the east, who has heard speak of it and does not fear. And master Edward Grim had seized him fast, and embraced him from beneath when they attacked him, and held him against them all, and was not terrified at anything, and had not let him go for the knights, though clerk and servant were all fled. Master Edward held him while they haled him. "What do you wish to do?" he said, "are you beside yourselves? Consider where you are, and what festival this is. It is a great sin to lay hand on your archbishop." But neither for festival nor for minster did they release him.

Now saw St Thomas well that his martyrdom was come. He put his hands to his face, and gave himself over to the Mother of God, to the martyr Denys, to whom sweet

> Ne[1] Deus ne voleit pas k'il fust traitiez vilment:
> S'il fist pur espruver cele malveise gent,
> S'osassent el mustier errer si cruelment.
> Car il n'a si felun, entrès k'en Orient,
> Qui en oï parler, qui ne s'en espoent.
>
> E mestre Edward Grim l'aveit forment saisi,
> Enbrascié par de sus, quant l'orent envaï;
> Cuntr'els tuz le retint, de rien ne s'esbahi,
> Ne pur les chevaliers ne l'aveit pas guerpi;
> Si clerc et si sergant[2] s'en èrent tuz fuï.
>
> Mestre Edward le tint kan k'il l'unt desachié:
> "Que volez, fet-il, fère? Estes-vus enragié?
> "Esguardez ù vus estes et qui sunt li feirié!
> "Main sur vostre arcevesque metez à grant pecchié!"
> Mès pur feirié ne l'unt[3], ne pur mustier lessié.
>
> Or veit bien saint Thomas sun martire en présent.
> Les mains mist á sun vis[4], à Dampnedeu se rent,
> Al martir saint Denis, cui dulce France apent,

---

[1] Mais, B.          [2] clerc e moine e sergant, B.
[3] Mais n'est pur nul feirié, B.
[4] Ses mains iuint à ses oilz, B.

France belongs; and to the saints of the church he commended himself incontinently—the cause of holy church and his own together. William stepped forward; nor was it in order to worship God. To be the lighter he would not wear a hauberk. He began to ask for the traitor to the king. When they could not cast the saint out of the minster, he sought to give him a great blow with the sword upon the head; so that he took off the top of his crown, and beat his pate down, and made a great hole in it. Upon his left shoulder glanced the sword, cut through the mantle and the clothes right to the skin, and clove the arm of Edward almost in two. Then at this blow Master Edward let go. "Strike!" then said William. But then Dan Reginald Fitzurse struck him, but did not beat him down. Then William de Tracy struck him again, and brained him altogether, and St Thomas fell. The felons returned to Saltwood. That night they boasted of their great felony.

> E as sainz de l'Yglise se commande erraument,
> La cause seinte Yglise et la sue ensement.
> Willames vint avant[1], ne volt Deu aorer.
> Pur estre plus legiers, n'i volt hauberc porter.
> Le traïtur le Rei commence à demander.
> Quant ne porent le saint hors del muster geter,
> Enz el chief de l'espée grant cop li va doner;
> Si ke de la corone le cupel en porta,
> Et la hure abati et granment entama.
> Sur l'espaulle senestre l'espée li cola,
> Le mantel et les dras très k'al quir encisa,
> E le bras Edward[2] près tut en dous colpa.
> Dunc l'aveit à cel colp mestre Edward guerpi.
> "Ferez," dunc fet Willames[3]. Mès idunc le féri
> Danz Renalz, le fils Hurs, mès pa ne l'abati.
> Idunc le referi Willames de Traci
> Qui tut l'escervela, et saint Thomas chaï.
> A Saltewode sunt li felun returné.
> De lur grant felunie se sunt la noit vanté,

[1] premiers, B.  [2] maistre Edward, B.
[3] "Ferez, ferez," fait il, B.

William de Tracy spoke and affirmed that he had cut off
the arm of John of Salisbury. By this we know that he had
wounded Master Edward—by this also that he was without
armour, followed him first of all, and was well known by
sight and voice; he had a green coat and a particoloured
cloak. When he saw that Reginald Fitzurse withdrew,
twice, as I have said, he smote the saint on the head.

But when Richard le Breton saw him thus beaten down,
and lying all outstretched upon the pavement, he struck
him a pound into the bargain on the other blows, so that
his shattered brand broke in two upon the stone. At the
Martyrdom they kiss the piece even now....

(p. 195, l. 21) Hugh de Morville was outside the choir;
he drove the people back who had come up. He was afraid
that the archbishop should then be taken from them. It
may be that he had bethought himself, and in this way
was keeping himself from his crime....

(p. 196, l. 6) Hugh Mauclerk, who came in after them,

> Willames de Traci a dit et afermé
> Johan de Salesbùre aveit le bras colpé:
> Pur ço savum qu'il ot mestre Edward nafré[1].
>    Pur ço k'iert desarmez tut primiers le siwi,
> Et bien fu conéuz et al vis et al cri;
> Une cote vert ot et mantel mi-parti.
> Quant il vit ke Renalz li filz Urs resorti,
> Dous feiz, si cum j'ai dit, le saint al chief feri.
>    Mès quant Richarz li Brez le vit si abatu,
> E sur le pavement gesir tut estendu,
> Un poi en bescoz l'a des autres cops feru,
> K'à la pière a brisié en dous sun brant molu.
> —Al martir beise-l'un la pièce tut à nu....
>    Huge de Moreville esteit ultre coruz;
> Chachout le pueple arère, ki esteit survenuz;
> Cremi ke l'arcevesques ne lur fust dunc toluz.
> Puet cel estre qu'il s'est en sei reconeüz;
> E de sa[2] felonie s'est issi defenduz....
>    E cil Huge Malclers, qui après els entra,

---

[1] B. puts this line first in the stanza.         [2] la, B.

set his foot on St Thomas's neck and dug; with the sword he cast the brain out of the head upon the pavement, and cried to them, "Let us get away, he will never rise again. "...

(l. 26) For the church of the north, and in the northern aisle, and turned toward the north, St Thomas suffered death....

The monks gathered up his blood and brain, and set them at his head in a pot, outside the tomb. (p. 199, l. 24) Before the high altar the holy body was carried, and there watched all the night by monks. The blood which had dripped from it was received....

(p. 202, l. 18) With great honour was he then buried in the crypt, for fear of the Brocks, lest he should be found. But now is he feared and honoured throughout the world.

Sur le col saint Thomas mist sun pié et ficha;
Le cervel od l'espée hors del chief li geta,
De sur le pavement, et à cels s'escria:
"Alun-nus en, fet-il, jà mès ne resurdra. "...
    Pur l'iglise del Nort, et el èle del Nort,
E vers le Nort turnez, suffri sainz Thomas mort[1]....
    Li moine en recuillirent le sanc et le cervel;
E à sun chief le mistrent en poz, hors del tumbel.
    Devant le grant[2] autel fu li cors sainz portez,
Et là de moines fu tute la noit guardez[3];
Recéuz fu li sancs ki en est degutez....
    A grant onur fu dunques ès crutes enterrez,
Pur poür des Brokeis, que il ne fust trovez.
—Mès or est par le mund cremuz et honurez.

# NOTE I

## THE WOUNDS

A careful reading of these narratives shows how difficult it is to say precisely how St Thomas came by his end. Who struck the first blow? How many blows did the saint receive? What

---

[1] Envers le nort, suffri li bons sainz Thomas mort, B.
[2] halt, B.
[3] E de moines e d'altres fu tute nuit guardez, B.

was the effect of each? To these questions different answers will
be given in accordance as one or another of the narrators is
considered to be the most trustworthy.

John of Salisbury may be at once dismissed. He mentions
no names, no one blow, and no number of blows. He mentions
only the saint's attitude—his bowed head—the cutting off of
the corona, which, so far as his narrative is concerned, might
have taken place by a deliberate act after St Thomas's death—
and the scattering of the brain.

William of Canterbury has no doubt that Reginald Fitzurse
struck the first blow (not counting the knocking off of the cap).
It was the only blow that William saw. Fitzurse was standing,
according to him, a little apart from the others, to the right, i.e.
apparently to Fitzurse's right, which would be Thomas's left.
It was a heavy blow. Fitzurse had stepped back for a moment,
apparently to obtain more freedom to strike. William heard
Fitzurse calling on the others to strike, but, fleeing at that moment, he saw no more. He did not know what effect the first
blow had. He knew, or was told, that there were other wounds
that followed. The later strokes, which he does not enumerate,
alighted, as he understood, on the part of the head where the
saint was already wounded by Fitzurse—*vulnera in vulnere*.
Then came the stroke which broke Le Breton's sword (though
William does not mention the name), and the outrage by Hugh
of Horsea (similarly unnamed). For all these later blows William is no original witness.

To a certain extent the narrative of Grim bears out the
account of William. He saw Fitzurse first brandish his sword
over St Thomas's head—which may have been the movement
that displaced the cap—and then spring suddenly at him and
strike. It was this first stroke, according to Grim, struck by
Fitzurse, which shore off the top of the saint's corona; and it
was the same stroke which wounded Grim himself. Grim does
not say at what point he left his master's side, as William does;
but it is natural to suppose that it was at this point, when he
could no longer be of use. If so, the remainder of his narrative
is not first-hand evidence. It is to the effect that a second blow
on the head left the martyr still standing, but that a third felled
him. Grim does not say who dealt these two blows nor anything about the character of them, but proceeds to the blow
which broke the sword. Of this blow he says that it severed the

corona (the top of which the first stroke had shorn off), to such an extent that the blood and brain came out—not a particularly lucid statement. He then mentions the outrage of Hugh, of which, following a system of comparison with the passion of our Lord, he makes a fifth wound, answering to that which pierced the heart of our Lord after death.

When we turn to Benedict, we must bear in mind that his narrative is not continuous, and that it has necessarily been to some extent adapted in order to work in with the rest of the narratives of the *Quadrilogus*. Otherwise his words "et ad alterum loricatum...dixit, 'Quid est, Reginalde?'" would imply that it was not Reginald who laid hold of Thomas and struck off his cap. A passage from William precedes these words in the *Quadrilogus*, referring to William de Tracy, and it may be assumed that Benedict agreed with William of Canterbury (and Grim) that it was Reginald's sword that was first flourished over the saint's head. The next fragment from Benedict speaks of a "second wound." No "first" wound has been mentioned in anything of Benedict's which has been preserved. In the *Quadrilogus* the "first" wound was inflicted by William de Tracy; we have no means of knowing to whom it was attributed by Benedict. But whereas Grim understood that the second stroke left St Thomas standing, Benedict says that it made him fall all along on the ground. Of the "third" he uses language which resembles Grim's language concerning his fourth; he says that it "cut off the greater part of his head, horribly enlarging the former wound." But it is not merely a difference of enumeration, for he clearly distinguishes this third blow from the fourth, which was the one that broke the sword. What is more curious is that Benedict explicitly ascribes to the author of the fourth blow (Le Breton, though he does not name him) the horrible act of Hugh of Horsea. He puts it down "eidem filio Sathanae."

The course of action in William Fitzstephen is different. The first blow, in his reckoning, was an act of warning. It was dealt with the flat of the sword, between the shoulders—no doubt over the head of the tall archbishop as he stooped. The first serious blow was the one which wounded Grim, as well as the archbishop; and it was dealt, not by Fitzurse, as Grim himself said, but by de Tracy. Fitzstephen gives an interesting reason for his belief that it was de Tracy who dealt it. It cut the head of the archbishop sufficiently to draw blood, but not much more. The next blow brought the archbishop to the ground. It was followed by Le Breton's stroke, which broke the sword, and by the act of Hugh of Horsea. Fitzstephen says that there were in all four strokes, all on the head. But he only specifies three, unless Hugh's outrage is intended to be the fourth, though it has not yet been mentioned at the point where the number four is given. Fitzstephen, like Grim and Benedict, speaks of the whole crown of the head as being cut off, but does not indicate when this was done.

Finally, Garnier, like Fitzstephen, makes de Tracy the striker of the first blow, giving the same ground for the identification as Fitzstephen, and adding further evidence on the point. It was this first blow which injured Grim; it made a great hole in the head of St Thomas, but yet glanced from the head to his left shoulder. The second blow was struck, almost at the same moment, by Fitzurse, but failed to bring St Thomas down. The third blow, like the first was de Tracy's, and this "brained" him. Then followed the stroke of Le Breton, and the act of Hugh of Horsea.

It may be worth while to add that Herbert of Bosham, who was not an eye-witness of the scene—for he had left Canterbury a few days before—but was usually well informed, agrees in the main with this order of things. It was William de Tracy, according to him, who struck the first blow, which wounded Grim, the spent force of the stroke coming down on St Thomas's head and drawing blood. After this, Herbert only speaks vaguely of blow after blow, the effect of which was at last to "sever the crown of the head from the head[1]." Herbert seems to have been unaware at what point in the tragedy the sword was broken: he describes it as being broken upon the martyr's head, not on the pavement, and at the same time breaking the skull; and curiously enough he attributes the atrocious act of Hugh, not to Hugh, but to the other clerical accomplice of the knights, Robert de Brock.

It is no great wonder that there are such discrepancies in the accounts, when we consider, not only the extreme agitation of the scene, but the darkness which must have prevailed at that

---

[1] Hinc inde feriunt et referiunt, feriunt inquam et referiunt, donec coronam capitis separarunt a capite.

hour in the low-vaulted transept. The day, it will be remembered, was December 29, and the hour that of the later evensong.

If we may now attempt to discern the facts contained in these confused narratives, the following points seem to be fairly certain. It was not the first stroke that killed St Thomas. Whether the striker was Fitzurse or de Tracy, the main force of it was spent on Edward Grim, and it did little injury to the archbishop. Nor was it the last stroke that killed him. If life was not already extinct, it must have been at the last flicker, and the stroke, if it touched him at all, could have done him as little harm as the first, for the violent contact with the floor must have warded it off from the prostrate man. Between these two strokes it is uncertain how many others reached him. Grim and Garnier had heard of one which reached him, but left him still on his feet. It was evidently not of a very serious character—if such a stroke there was. The blow which followed in Grim and Garnier—the second blow in Fitzstephen and Benedict—brought the martyr to the ground, and was in all probability the death-blow. Grim, it is true, makes him murmur certain words after his fall, but they are only a partial repetition of words uttered earlier. The striker of this stroke, according to Garnier, was William de Tracy. It penetrated to the brain; according to the same writer, it "tut l'escervela[1]."

One fact of some importance for this enquiry seems well established. It is that as soon as the struggle round the pillar ceased, St Thomas bent his head, and held it steadily in position for the murderers to strike. A swordsman who has freedom of action would naturally, if he is not left-handed, raise his sword over his own right shoulder, and would naturally strike the head of the man opposite to him on the left side. If the stroke were forcible enough to bring the man down, he would naturally fall on his right side. This is what St Thomas did. Benedict says that he lay on his right side. So far, this is in favour of supposing that the blow came from the left.

A second point to be observed is that almost all the authorities relate that the "crown" of St Thomas's head was especially injured. The "crown" was not what a modern Englishman might naturally take to be meant. It was the part of the head

[1] The blows and wounds may be tabulated thus (see overleaf):

which had received the tonsure and the unction. When Grim mentions that the "crown" of St Thomas's head was "large," he does not refer to the size or proportions of the saint's head, but to the fact that the barber had shaven a particularly large part of it. This shaven part of St Thomas's head has an important place in the saint's posthumous history, as we shall see. But it is by no means clear what happened to it at the time of the martyrdom. William of Canterbury does not mention it. William Fitzstephen says that "the whole crown of the head

| William of Canterbury | Benedict | William Fitzstephen | Grim | Garnier | Herbert of Bosham |
|---|---|---|---|---|---|
| Fitzurse knocks off cap | (? Fitzurse) knocks off cap | Someone strikes St T. with flat sword | Fitzurse brandishes sword over him | | |
| Fitzurse strikes first blow | [Missing] | De Tracy strikes first blow, wounding Grim | Fitzurse strikes first blow, wounding Grim | De Tracy strikes first blow, wounding Grim | De Tracy strikes first blow, wounding Grim |
| | | | "Another blow" leaves St T. standing | Fitzurse strikes, but St T. still stands | |
| [Further "wounds on the wound"] | "Second" blow brings St T. to the ground | "Second" blow brings St T. to the ground | "Third" blow brings him to the ground | De Tracy brings him to the ground | [Blow after blow] |
| | "Third" blow severs great part of head | [Four strokes, all in head] | [Five wounds] | | |
| Sword broken on pavement (no name) | Sword broken on pavement (no name) | Le Breton's sword broken on pavement | Sword broken on pavement (no name) | Le Breton's sword broken on pavement | Sword broken on St T.'s head (no name) |
| Head pierced (no name) | Head pierced by same man | Head pierced by Hugh of Horsea | Head pierced by Hugh of Horsea | Head pierced by Hugh of Horsea | Head pierced by Robert de Brock |

was cut off," and that Hugh drew out the brain "from the cavity of the severed crown"; he speaks of "what was left" of the head after this mutilation. Edward Grim says that the stroke by which he was himself wounded "shore off the top of his crown"; but he supposes that the final stroke, when the archbishop was prostrate, "so severed the crown from the head" as to mingle the brain with the blood. Benedict affirms that when the martyr was on the ground, one man—not Le Breton, who is separately mentioned—"cut off the greater part of his head,"—this being an "enlargement" of a former wound. John of Salisbury implies that it was after the archbishop's death that "they cut off the crown of his head." Garnier only mentions that the "cupel" was taken off from the crown. Herbert, as we have seen, considers that the result of blow after blow was to "sever the crown of the head from the head."

At a later time the language of Benedict (who may be called the standard authority) was taken literally, as probably he intended it to be taken, and it was thought that the greater part of St Thomas's head was sliced off, bone and all. The well-known glass painting in Lincoln Minster shows it. But besides the inherent difficulty of slicing off with a sword the greater part of the head of a man lying on a stone pavement, and besides the visible weakness of Benedict's language at that point, there is some direct evidence to show that Benedict was wrong. When the martyr's body was laid out before the high altar, and when it was transferred next morning to its tomb in the crypt, opportunity was given for observing the condition of the head. The opportunity was not wholly lost. William Fitzstephen gives some information about the head which has all the appearance of truth. He tells how the archbishop's chamberlain, before the body was moved from the Martyrdom, bound up the wounded head with a strip of his own clothing. He tells how, at the high altar, the skull, with its gaping wound, was seen covered with a clean linen cloth, and how, over this again, the close-fitting cap, which had been knocked off in the scuffle, served as an additional bandage. It would not be easy to fit such a cap upon a head of which so large a portion had been amputated. To this account of Fitzstephen Benedict adds a note about the appearance of the as yet unbandaged head. There was, he says, a kind of circlet of blood round the head—that is, probably, on the tonsured part of the head. No eye-witness could have described thus a head from which the whole top had been severed, unless indeed the severed part had been very neatly fitted on again. In spite of what he had said before about the greater part of the head being cut off, he now records only a red mark round this part. Neither he, nor Fitzstephen, nor any of the others, relates that an amputated portion was picked up and either put in place again or dealt with separately. That the blood, the brains, were gathered up, is carefully recorded; but not a word in the foregoing historians indicates that any detached portion of skin and skull was found;—that such a portion was found and treated separately, as the blood was, seems definitely excluded[1].

It is true that John of Salisbury speaks in a general way of the ground being strewn "with bones" as well as blood, but the expression cannot be taken literally, although it finds a measure of support in a document which we have now to consider.

The fullest account of the wounded head, given by any contemporary, is that of Gervase. It is not probable that Gervase witnessed the act of Richard le Breton. His description of what Le Breton did agrees in the main with that of Benedict, and doubtless represents the views of the convent. But Gervase adds details which are not found elsewhere, and that Gervase saw the body after the murder is certain[2].

"One of them, more inhumanly savage than the rest, as [Thomas] lay there at the point of death, cut off the *testulae* of his head, which [*testulae*] others had cloven; and so easy was the passage [through the skull thus opened] that the contact with the pavement broke the point of his sword. The wound ran down from the apex of the head as far as to the *cella memorialis*, laying that part of the hind-head open. Finally a

---

[1] The earliest notice of what was done with the *corona* occurs in the Iceland Saga (Vol. I. p. 554): "Then they lay the body on a hand-bier, and sew to the head, as well as might be, what was cut off of the crown, and then wash the face." From what source the Saga derived the statement is not known. The surrounding narrative is not trustworthy: e.g. it relates that the body was carried down to the crypt for the night, to the altar of St John the Baptist and St Austin, whereas it was certainly laid before the high altar in the choir.

[2] Gerv. *Acta Pontificum* (Rolls Series), Vol. II. p. 396: quod oculis meis vidi et manibus attrectavi, habet ad carnem cilicium.

certain Hugh Mauclerk, who well deserved the name, stepped up, and atrociously drove the point of his sword into the gaping head, broke up the brain altogether, drew it out, and scattered it with *testulae* and blood upon the pavement[1]."

A little further on Gervase adds:

"The sacred blood, with the brain and *testulae*, was collected and carefully laid up, to be administered later on to the whole world[2]."

Gervase's testimony seems, perhaps, rather clearer than it really is. We must examine it with care. The language is only in part technical. The *conus capitis*, no doubt, means the top of the head. My kind friends Professor Sir Clifford Allbutt and Professor Macalister, whom I have consulted, tell me that no book exists which deals with the technical terms of mediaeval surgery; and I cannot find that *conus* was used in any specialised sense in the medical science of Gervase's time. We are therefore thrown back upon the natural use of the word as it occurs in earlier days. The *Thesaurus Linguae Latinae* gives, for instance, the gloss of Servius upon *Aeneid* iii. 468, "Conus est curvatura quae in galea prominet, super quam cristae sunt." Solinus uses it of the crest of the phoenix. Cyprianus Gallus uses it of the top or crest of a palm tree. Evidently Gervase means the highest part of the head—the part from which the crest of a helmet would spring.

*Cella memorialis*, on the other hand, is highly technical. Ludovicus Vives *de Anima* II. (in the ed. of his works published at Valencia, 1782, tom. III. p. 346) gives the following ingenious account of the "seat of memory":

"Memoriae sedes, ac velut fabrica, in occipitio est a natura

---

[1] Gerv. *Chronica* (Rolls Series), p. 227: Quidam autem ex eis immanior caeteris et inhumanior, jam jacentis, jam expirantis testulas capitis quas alii inciderant abscidit, et ex facili transitu pavimentum offendens gladii cuspidem fregit. Plaga autem, a cono capitis usque ad cellam memorialem descendens, partem illam occipitii patulam fecit. Accessit postremo quidam Hugo, re et nomine Malus-clericus appellatus, ensis cuspidem patenti capiti crudeliter impressit, cerebrum penitus dissipavit, extraxit et in pavimentum cum testulis et sanguine sparsit.

[2] *Ibid.* p. 228: Collectus est ille sacrosanctus sanguis cum cerebro et testulis, et diligenter repositus est, post modicum toti mundo propinandus. On p. 229 Gervase speaks of seeing "interiora capitis tam dire dissipati."

collocata, admirabili sapientia, quod praeterita cernat ; ita illic velut oculum habemus quendam multo praestantiorem, quam si corporalis aliquis esset astructus, qualis in fronte: quod in fabulis est de Iano."

Sir Clifford Allbutt writes to me:

"I have consulted Professor Macalister on the point, and he says the fourth ventricle of the brain was called the *cella memoriae*—especially its cerebellar recess. Likewise the occipital bone, which lies near it, was called the *os memoriae*."

A greater difficulty lies in determining what Gervase meant by the word *testulae*. It looks at first sight as if this were another technical term. *Testa* (tête) is used for a skull—first a dry skull —then a head. *Testula* or the plural *testulae* might have been used to describe a particular part of the skull. But of this I can find no trace. In fact, the connexion of the word in this passage with *testa* in the sense of "head" appears to be altogether accidental. The word goes back to the earlier meaning of *testa*, a piece of earthenware. *Testa* itself is often used in the sense of a *broken* piece of earthenware, a potsherd—in this sense it occurs in the Vulgate (e.g. Job ii. 8, of the potsherd which Job used to scrape himself withal). From this it came to be used of other broken bits of similar material. Celsus uses *testa* of any bone, like those of the arm or leg even when not broken (viii. 16: "in omnibus membris longis, quae per articulum longa testa iunguntur"), and of fragments of bone (vii. 12, 1: "scire licet aliquid ex osse fractum esse. ergo specillo conquirenda est testa quae recessit, et vulsella protrahenda est. si non sequitur, incidi gingiva debet, donec labans ossis testa recipiatur"; cp. vi. 13: "testa ossis, si qua recessit, recipienda est"), and of the splinters of a tooth (vi. 9: "baca hederae...dentem findit, isque per testas excidit"). It is from this sense of *testa* that *testula* in Gervase is derived. So far from indicating a special portion of the anatomy of a skull, it has nothing to do with a skull at all, but only means a broken bit, a splinter of bone. From the context it is plain that the splinters in question were splinters of St Thomas's skull, but the word itself does not imply it.

Where Gervase's account fails to help us is in not saying along what part of the circumference of the skull, his line ran between the "cone of the head" and "that part of the hind-head" where memory dwelt. The natural impression would be that it clove the skull down the middle. "The wound," Dr Macalister concluded, "sliced open the back of the skull above the nape of the neck." If this is so, it would be fatal to the claim of the bones discovered in 1888 to be the bones of St Thomas. They have not been cloven in the way described. But the description would be equally fatal to the chief argument against the claim. A stroke which clove the skull along the middle could hardly cut anything off it. The famous *corona* might be divided or broken to pieces by such a cut; it could not be severed from the head. It is difficult also to see how a sword lighting upon a head in that direction could be supposed to reach the pavement, as Gervase says, through the wound. To give any sense to Gervase's language, we must, I think, understand him to mean that the line of the wound "ran down" along one side of the head, or the other side, between the points mentioned. According to the evidence the dead or dying man lay on his right side. In this way the left side of the skull, which had already been cloven by the blow which felled him, would again receive the first impact —probably from the handle-half of the sword, as the point snapped off on the stone. This would allow for the "enlargement" of the wound (to use Benedict's expression), and for the hacking off of *testulae*, chips and splinters of bone, and make it easier for the last assailant to strew the ground with them.

It will be observed that Gervase gives no specific information with regard to the *corona* which is supposed to have been severed. If any part of the bony structure was cut off, which could be described as the *corona*, to Gervase it was only one of several *testulae*, or broken bits. Clearly it cannot have been a large piece, attracting marked attention. If it had, he could hardly have failed to speak of it separately. From his silence we should judge either that the *corona*, if detached at all, was put on again and buried with the rest of the head, as the Iceland Saga affirms, or that the name was afterwards given to one of the precious chips, which at the time had nothing very remarkable about it to distinguish it from the rest.

# NOTE II

## SOME TOPOGRAPHICAL DETAILS

### A.

### *The Archbishop's Palace*

So few pieces of the mediaeval *palatium ecclesiae* are left, that any attempt to give a plan of it as it was in 1170 must be largely conjectural. Willis's plan is so. So is the one in this volume.

For readers who only know modern Canterbury, it may be useful to premise that the main approach to the mediaeval palace was not, like that to the modern house, through the south or Christ Church gate, but from Palace Street, on the western side. So, it may be added, was the approach to all the busy life of the convent. Visitors to the cathedral church ordinarily entered, as they do now, by the Christ Church gate, and by the south door. But all visitors and business people coming to the convent entered by the great gate leading from what is now called the Mint Yard into the *curia*, or Green Court. All visitors or business people coming to the archbishop's house came in by his great gate from Palace Street. The archway of it still stands, with an interesting chamber over it, in the occupation of Messrs Gibbs, the printers. The existing archway is later than the time of St Thomas, but it doubtless occupies the same site as the gateway concerned with his history.

Opposite this gateway, as we learn from Fitzstephen—that is, on the other side of Palace Street—was a big house which served the murderers for a rendezvous. The gateway, like all important gateways, was furnished with a wicket; whether cut through the main door or architecturally separate, we are not informed.

This great gateway led first into a large court or yard (*curia, atrium aulae, curtis*), bounded to the north by a wall which fenced the approach to the convent gate, where "the Grange" is now; to the east by the Pentise running up to the Cellarer's Hall and by that Hall itself; and to the west by Palace Street. Doubtless there were buildings of various kinds at points along these boundaries. The stables would seem to have adjoined the gate[1]. Presumably it was close to these stables that Fitz-nigel, in William Fitzstephen's narrative, stood among the horses "in front of the gate." The mulberry tree—it is interesting to read of a mulberry tree in England at that date—under which the knights threw off their cloaks, appears to have stood somewhere in this court.

The southern side of this courtyard, or the greater part of that side, was occupied by the big hall (*aula*) of the house. This hall with its dependent buildings is what William of Canterbury calls the outer house (*exterior domus*). It was not entered immediately from the courtyard, but through a vestibule or porch-room (called by Fitzstephen the *proaulum*, or fore-hall), in which Fitzurse armed himself. Of this fore-hall, as well as of the hall itself, interesting portions remain, though they belong to Stephen Langton's rebuilding of the house. In the angle of the west wall of the fore-hall with the north wall of the hall is a winding staircase. This, or rather its Norman predecessor, would seem to have been the staircase (then of wood) where Fitz-stephen wrongly supposed that Fitzurse found his axe.

Through the *aula* people passed into the "inner house" (*interior domus*)[2]. This was a building of two storeys, if not more. Robert de Brock and the knights were obliged to use a ladder, in default of the interrupted stairs to the side door, in order to reach the level of the window by which they broke in. Either the outside walls or the inside partitions were, at any rate in places, of wood:—St Thomas and his companions could hear Robert hacking at a certain *paries*, to force an entrance to the *interiora domus*[3]. The paper printed by Willis, which has been referred to above, mentions two chambers adjoining the great hall—presumably to the south—and beyond these "a great chamber," which had a kitchen of its own. This great chamber was probably where St Thomas had just dined when the knights arrived. The paper speaks also of "my lord's little chamber" (*camera domini parva*), which must be supposed to have been the chamber to which St Thomas had withdrawn after dinner

---

[1] See the (later) document in Willis, *Conventual Buildings of Christ Church*, p. 190: "Item porta magna cum stablis indiget magna re-paracione."

[2] The knights in Fitzstephen run out from St Thomas's room "per medium aulae et atrii."

[3] Fitzstephen. Grim, however, calls it only a *ligneum obstaculum*, which might mean a door.

for business. It might have been thought that he had dined in the hall, and retired to the great "chamber." This supposition would be favoured, both by the number of persons who seem to have attended him in the *thalamus,* and by the stress which seems to be laid upon his accompanying the knights "all the way to the door[1]." But the question is settled by Garnier's statement that St Thomas made all his people "en la grant chambre entrer[2]" when he thought of seeing the knights in private. No doubt "my lord's little chamber" opened out of the big one. It was probably his sleeping chamber as well as study. The Auctor Anonymus I. represents St Thomas as sitting upon "his bed" in the same chamber after the interview[3]. The windows of the room appear to have opened towards the church, because something of what was going on in the church could be heard from it[4]. Adjoining "my lord's chamber," St Thomas had constructed a second large hall, known afterwards as "beati Thomae aula[5]."

The knights were led by Robert to the attack from the garden or orchard (*virgultum, pomerium*). This, to one entering the premises from the gate and courtyard, was beyond the big hall first mentioned—i.e. beyond the *exterior domus*. It must have occupied the ground to the west and south of the hall and of the dwelling-house. The way to it led past the kitchen[6]. This kitchen was probably the square building marked on Willis's plan near the west end of the hall, now used as a class room for the Junior Department of the King's School. Square kitchens were the rule, and they were generally detached, or semi-detached, from the residential apartments. The attack upon the house must have been from the west. If the knights and their men had been on the eastern side of the house, between it and the Cellarer's lodgings, they would have intercepted the archbishop and his company before he reached the

[1] William of Canterbury: "usque ad ostium."

[2] Garnier, p. 182.

[3] *Materials,* Vol. IV. p. 74: "Reversus...ad suos, sedit supra lectum suum." The "suum" seems to show that the "lectus" was not a couch for use in the day time. Perhaps the *ostium* to which St Thomas accompanied the knights was that of the "great chamber."

[4] Fitzstephen.

[5] Willis, p. 190: "domus magna que vocatur aula b. Thome juxta cameram domini."

[6] Garnier, p. 188: "Par de vers la cusine sunt entré el vergier."

cloister, and would have slain him there. A side door (*posticium* —Garnier calls it *un oriol*) led down by steps from the door of the "outer chamber" to the orchard[1].

The usual way for the archbishop and his household to get to church was either through the courtyard and so through the convent, or by a door, the existence of which may be assumed, in the south wall of the garden, giving access to the great west door of the church, and to the little north-west door of the nave and the adjoining gate of the cloister. But these ways were stopped by the enemy, and they were forced to try another[2].

Willis[3] has given convincing reasons for thinking that the door which was so easily forced for St Thomas was not the door of the cloister itself. This, as he says, "must have been in constant use by the servants of the convent." If it was usually fastened, as probably it was, the fastening would be on the cellarer's side, and easily removed. Benedict seems to make the matter clear. There were two doors which caused anxiety. One was in the archbishop's house itself, the other the (still existing) door into the cloister at the north-west corner. The difficulty with the second was that the archbishop and his men had not got the key; but the cellarer's servants heard them coming and set the door open before they came. The first, in the archbishop's house[4], had been so long unused[5] that they feared lest the bolts should stick through rust or what not—or perhaps the key was lost. Garnier[6] makes it clear that this door was in the house:

[1] Benedict. Anon. I. p. 75, says: "ascendit...Robertus per deambulatorium, quod ibi de veteri tunc renovabatur, ut aperiret ostia." Garnier's words are: "Al us (i.e. ostium) de la chaumbre out un oriol fermé."

[2] Anon. I. p. 75, says: "Circumspicientes autem viderunt *curiam* plenam armatis, et *pomerium*, viasque quibus ad ecclesiam pergebatur praeoccupatas militibus."

[3] *Conventual Buildings*, pp. 116, 117. On p. 116, l. 4, Willis has put "south" by an obvious slip for "north."

[4] Grim calls it "ostium per quod iter erat in claustrum monachorum," which would not naturally describe a door giving immediate admittance to the cloister.

[5] Grim: "multis ante diebus diligenter obseratum." Cp. Anon. I. p. 75: "quod multo tempore clausum et obseratum nulli transitum praebuerat."

[6] P. 189.

As autres chaumbres out une chambre ajustée,
Par où la veie esteit al cloistre plus privée;
Mès à cel ore esteit à un grand loc fermée.
Mult en fu esbaïe la gent chaperunée,
Quand virent si lur veie totes parz estopée.

## B.

### *The Martyrdom Transept*

The walls of the western transepts and of the nave still stand
on the foundations laid by Lanfranc; and in the Martyrdom
transept the lower courses of Lanfranc's work still appear in
one place inside the church, namely beneath Dr Chapman's
monument. The turret in the north-west corner is likewise part
of Lanfranc's building, up to the string course to be seen at
the level of the Norman roof, and contains the actual stairway
up which Fitzstephen says that St Thomas could easily have
escaped, if he had wished. These portions of the transept
witnessed the tragedy, and so did the great Norman pier of the
central tower, of which a part of the capital has recently been
allowed to look out again upon the scene through a slit in its
fifteenth-century casing.

All else, however, is changed; and it requires an effort to
imagine what the transept was then like.

In the first place the floor-space was much larger than it is
now. The reason for this is that the great flight of steps up to
the eastern part of the church was not then so wide as it is now.
It now includes nearly the whole width of the north aisle; then
it was not wider than the nave. The main way from the north
transept to the north aisle of the choir was up a flight of steps
corresponding to that which still leads from the south transept
to the south aisle of the choir. The downward termination of
this flight may be inferred by observing how Prior Ernulph's
diaper ends on the wall between the tunnel and the crypt steps.
There was also a way from the transept to reach the west entrance to the choir, but it stood further south than the present
steps, and corresponded to those that now lead from the south
transept to the space under the lantern. In Gervase's time this
latter way, on the south side of the tower, had only lately been
opened, but the northern approach—the monks' usual approach
—was as old as the time of St Anselm, if not of Lanfranc.

Gervase's language makes this clear. After saying that one description would do for the two transepts, he proceeds to describe the southern one thus:

"Between this chapel[1] [St Michael's] and the choir the space is divided into two; that is to say, into the few steps by which you go into the crypt, and the many by which you reach the upper parts of the church."

Then of the northern transept he says in like manner:

"Between the chapel [St Benet's] and the choir the space is divided into two; that is to say, into the steps which go down into the crypt and the steps which go up and lead to the eastern parts of the church....From this transept to the tower, and from the tower to the choir, you go up by many steps. From the tower you go down into the south transept by a new door. From the tower you go down also into the nave by two gates[2]."

St Thomas, on entering the Martyrdom, had thus the choice of two ways *ad aram superius*[3]. There is no doubt that he chose the one leading to the north aisle. Garnier, who could not have been mistaken on this point, says that the pillar, of which we shall have to speak, hid him from the knights as they entered[4]. A glance at the plan will show that this could not have happened if he had taken the steps that led into the tower space. This supposition explains also the statement of Grim that he turned to the right to this pillar on reaching the floor level. He did not wish the pillar to be between him and the knights at the door.

The pillar of which mention is so often made stood, no doubt, in the line of the outside wall of the church, midway between the

---

[1] Willis, *Canterbury Cathedral*, p. 39, gives reasons for translating *porticus* by the word "apse"; but these chapels, at any rate, were more than apses—they were chapels with apsidal ends.

[2] Gervase, *Opera Historica* (Rolls Series), Vol. I. pp. 10, 11: "Utrarumque istarum una fere est descriptio....Inter hanc porticum [S. Michaelis] et chorum spatium est in duo divisum, scilicet in gradus paucos per quos itur in criptam, et in gradus multos per quos ad superiora ecclesiae pervenitur....Inter porticum [S. Benedicti] et chorum spatium est in duo divisum, scilicet in gradus qui in criptam descendunt, et in gradus qui ad partes ecclesiae orientales ascendentes transmittunt....De hac cruce in turrem, de turre in chorum per gradus plurimos ascenditur. Descenditur vero de turre per ostium novum in crucem australem. Item de turre descenditur in navem per duos valvas."—The *duo valvae* were behind the Rood Altar.

[3] Fitzstephen.        [4] See above, p. 39.

piers carrying the second bay of the transept. There was a similar one in the south transept. Gervase says:

"Each transept had in the midst of it a stout pillar, which carried a vault starting from the walls on three sides of it[1]."

The second *sui* in the sentence of Gervase refers to the pillar. The walls from which the vault proceeded can have been no other than the west, north, and east walls of the transept itself; on the fourth side, towards the tower there was no wall. The pillar carried, not merely "a gallery leading to the chapel of St Blaise[2]," but an upper floor to the whole part of the transept projecting beyond the nave wall. This part of the transept was thus divided horizontally in two. A similar arrangement existed in several churches in Normandy, to which Stanley rightly refers, and particularly in St Stephen's at Caen, which was Lanfranc's model for his cathedral at Canterbury. Stanley's "gallery," from which "draperies and curtains could be hung," was erected after the removal of the pillar and the vault[3]. The level of the upper floor may still be observed from the transept by a slight bend in the turret about the height of the adjacent window sills. The staircase in the wall of the north choir aisle led to it; and on the staircase of the turret at the same height two steps that are rounded off, and joints in the masonry, show where a way in the thickness of the wall led to a door which must have been immediately over the door of the turret still existing on the ground level.

Gervase defines the exact place of the martyrdom:

"Between this space [i.e. the space occupied by the stairs to the crypt and to the choir aisle] and the chapel [of St Benedict] is a solid wall, in front of which...St Thomas...fell. This place of martyrdom was opposite to the cloister door....The pillar which had stood in the middle of this transept, and the vault which rested upon it, were demolished in course of time, in reverence for the martyr, in order that the altar erected on the place of the martyrdom might be more freely seen[4]."

---

[1] Utraque in medio sui pilarium fortem habebat, qui fornicem a parietibus prodeuntem in tribus sui partibus suscipiebat.

[2] Stanley.

[3] Gervase's words after speaking of the removal of the vault are: In circum vero ad altitudinem fornicis praedictae via quaedam facta est qua pallia et cortinae possint suspendi.

[4] "Inter hoc spatium et praedictam porticum murus solidus est, ante quem...Sanctus...Thomas...occubuit....Hic locus martyrii ex

The altar of which Gervase here speaks was the altar of the Sword's Point. No altar stood against that solid wall when St Thomas fell in front of it. The nearest was the altar of St Benedict. It is this—not, as is often supposed, the *altare ad Punctum Ensis*—which figures so frequently in the mediaeval pictures and sculptures of the scene. Over the south door of the cathedral itself still stands the carved representation of a draped altar, as if the martyrdom had taken place at it, though the effigies of the saint and his murderers have long vanished. It was, of course, by an artistic licence that the tragedy was placed so near it[1].

St Thomas, standing at his pillar with his back to it, and facing the door, was placed between the altar of St Benedict on his right hand, and that of the Lady Chapel on his left. This is clearly pointed out by Garnier, and by Grim. Fitzstephen only mentions that the altar of St Benedict was close by. William of Canterbury on the other hand speaks of St Thomas as having his back to the wall—that is, the wall where the altar of the Sword's Point afterwards stood—and facing the image of the Blessed Virgin. The Lady Chapel of the Norman church occupied the east end of the north aisle of the nave. The image probably stood over the altar, looking down upon it. There was no access from the Lady Chapel to the transept except by way of the tower. From the language of Garnier we might infer that the level of the chapel, and consequently of the nave, was lower than that of the transept; but of this there is no other indication, and probably he only means that the chapel was nearer to what we naturally call the bottom of the church, that is, the west end.

The altar for which St Thomas was making was not the high altar of the choir, but that of the Trinity Chapel to the east of it.

opposito habuit ostium claustri....Pilarius autem ille qui in medio crucis hujus steterat, et fornix ei innitens, processu temporis ob reverentiam martyris demolita sunt, ut altare in loco martyrii elevatum ampliori spatio cerneretur." Gervase was writing about fifteen years after the martyrdom.

[1] A nice example of such pictures is given by Dr Abbott as the frontispiece to his *St Thomas of Canterbury*, Vol. I. Several are given in Dr Dearmer's *Fifty Pictures of Gothic Altars* (Alcuin Club Collections, X), nos. VIII, IX, XXIII, XXIV, XXX, XXXV, XL, XLIV. The one at the head of the tomb of King Henry IV is all but perished, but the copy hung near it tells the story.

This square chapel is clearly marked in Willis's plan of the Norman church, p. 38. The parallel between the language of Fitzstephen (see above, p. 16) and that of Gervase (i. 16, Rolls Series) is very close. Gervase speaking of the Trinity chapel says:

"Capella vero extra murum posita, eidem tamen conjuncta et ad orientem porrecta, altare habebat Sanctae Trinitatis; ubi beatus martyr Thomas die consecrationis suae primam missam celebravit. In hac capella, ante exilium et post, missas celebrare, horas audire, et frequenter orare solebat."

It will be remembered that the conventual evensong was finished, or nearly so, by the time St Thomas entered the church. The Icelandic Saga (Rolls Series, Vol. i. p. 534) gives the interesting information that "the church of Canterbury has two services sung every day, that is to say, that of the monks and that of the clerks." The object of the writer in mentioning the fact is apparently, as Dr Abbott remarks (*St Thomas of Canterbury*, i. 41), to show that the archbishop was not late for vespers. He was going to the second service, which evidently took place in the Trinity chapel.

The Dean of Wells has kindly sent me the following illustrations of Fitzstephen's *missae familiares*.

EADMER, *Vita Anselmi*, lib. i. § 16 (Migne, clviii. 58):

After the death of his pupil Osbern for a whole year Anselm celebrated mass every day. "Quod si aliquando a celebratione ipsius sacramenti impediebatur, eos qui missas *familiares* debebant suam pro anima fratris missam dicere faciebat; et ipse missas eorum, dum opportunum erat, ante missam sui defuncti alia missa persolvebat."

[It is interesting to note that this duplication was not then forbidden.]

PECKHAM'S CONSTITUTIONS, Council of Lambeth, Oct. 1181 (Wilkins, ii. 52):

"*De annualibus et anniversariis celebrandis.*

"Sacerdotes insuper caveant universi ne missarum peculiarium seu *familiarium* se celebrationi obligent, quo minus valeant canonico officio commissam sibi ecclesiam officiare ut tenentur."

Other references in Du Cange (s.v. missa) show that *missa familiaris* is a private mass (e.g. *pro familiaribus vel benefactoribus*) in contrast to *missa publica*.

# SECTION II

## THE TOMB AND THE SHRINE

# SECTION II

## THE TOMB AND THE SHRINE

OUR next duty is to trace, as far as may be possible, the history of the relics of St Thomas from the day of his burial—December 30, 1170—to the reign of Henry VIII. The special object will be to determine whether the bones were all kept together, or separated and differently dealt with.

### A. THE TOMB.

Miracles began to take place immediately after the martyrdom. Some were wrought at a distance, through the invocation of the saint; some through drinking water tinged with an infusion of his blood. The church had been desecrated by the murder, and was shut up; but at Easter, 1171, the doors were opened, and sufferers were allowed to have access to the tomb[1]. This caused a great increase in the number of miracles, and it was reported that some of those who had been concerned in the murder were once more thinking of coming and carrying the body off.

[Benedict, p. 77] "For the sake of security we arrayed forces in opposition; but we also removed the body of the saint from its marble tomb into a wooden coffin, and hid it behind the altar of St Mary[2], in order that if the wicked should by any chance prevail, they might retire disappointed and confounded on finding that the martyr was not in his sepulchre[3]."

[1] Benedict, *Materials*, II. pp. 35, 60.
[2] That is, St Mary of the Undercroft, not the one near the Martyrdom.
[3] Securitatis causa parantur a nobis vires contrariae; sed et corpus sancti de tumba marmorea in capsam ligneam transponentes retro altare beatae Mariae abscondimus, quatenus si forte viribus praevalerent maligni, martyrem in sepulcro non invenientes, fraudati redirent atque confusi.

It will be observed that Benedict gives no hint that any part of the body was abstracted.

The next day, the plot having been defeated by a storm, one or two remarkable miracles took place at this new resting place of the saint.

[Benedict, p. 81] "Seeing therefore how God multiplied His mercy with us, and knowing that this wealth of signs and wonders fomented the hatred and envy of the malignant, lest they should attempt a second time what they had before been unable to accomplish, we laid the martyr again in the former place, and made the sepulchre sure, sealing the stone and setting a watch. There was erected around the marble sarcophagus a wall of great hewn stones, very firmly cramped together with mortar and iron and lead, with two windows in either side, at which those who came might insert their heads and be able to reach and kiss the sarcophagus; and a large marble slab was laid over it likewise; and the structure was hollow between the top of the sarcophagus and the slab over it, giving an interval of nearly a foot. Several curious things happened in connexion with those windows, which deserve to be told[1]."

Far the most wonderful event that happened there, though it does not fall in with Benedict's scheme to record it, was the penance performed by King Henry II in 1174, when he inserted his head in one of these openings and received the lash. There are many pictures of the tomb

---

[1] Videntes ergo quantum multiplicaret nobiscum misericordiam suam Deus, scientesque quod haec signorum et prodigiorum copia odii et invidiae fomitem malignantibus administraret, ne forte rursum attentarent quod ante perficere nequiverant, martyrem in locum priorem reponentes munivimus sepulcrum, signantes lapidem cum custodibus. Erectus est autem circa sarcophagum marmoreum paries de lapidibus magnis sectis, caemento et ferro et plumbo firmissime consolidatis, duas in utroque laterum habens fenestras, quibus advenientes capitibus immissis ad osculum sarcophagi pervenire valerent, superposita nihilominus tabula grandi marmorea; eratque structura concava inter sarcophagi summitatem et tabulam superpositam, paene pedalem habens distantiam. De fenestris autem admiranda quaedam contigerunt et digna relatu.

and its "windows" in the glass of St Thomas's chapel in the cathedral.

## B. THE TRANSLATION.

The body of St Thomas remained in the *tumba* in the crypt for fifty years. The choir of the church overhead was destroyed in the great fire of 1174, and rebuilt. In 1179 William the Englishman "laid the foundation for the enlargement of the church at the eastern part, because a chapel of St Thomas was to be built there[1]." In the following summer, "the outer wall round the chapel of St Thomas, begun before the winter, was elevated as far as the turning of the vault. But the master had begun a tower at the eastern part outside the circuit of the wall, as it were, the lower vault of which was completed before the winter[2]." "The chapel of the Holy Trinity...was then levelled to the ground; this had hitherto remained untouched out of reverence to St Thomas, who was buried in the crypt [of it][3]." The altar at which he said his first mass was transferred to the chapel of St John in the south-east transept. "The translation of St Thomas was reserved until the completion of his chapel. For it was fitting...that such a translation should be most solemn and public. In the meantime, therefore, a wooden chapel, sufficiently decent for the place and occasion, was prepared around and above his tomb[4]." Gervase records in summary fashion the progress of the building as far as the year 1184. The new crypt, enclosing the wooden chapel, was completed in 1181, and the vaulting of the great chapel above, together with that of the *corona*, three years later. There his invaluable history stops.

The documents which follow describe the translation of St Thomas to his new resting place in 1220. Of these, the first is the *Polistorie*[5]. The *Polistorie* is a

---

[1] Gervase, in Willis, *Canterbury Cathedral*, p. 51.
[2] *Ibid.* p. 56. The "tower" was the *corona*.
[3] *Ibid.* p. 56.  [4] *Ibid.* p. 58.
[5] Not *Polistoire*, as Stanley writes it.

Canterbury Chronicle in French, down to the death of Robert Winchelsea, and the enthronement of his successor in 1313. From what contemporary source it draws the account of the translation I cannot say, but the account bears the stamp of accuracy. A great part of the passage has been printed, with some slight errors, in Stanley's *Memorials of Canterbury*, Appendix, Note 1[1].

## (1) *The Polistorie.*

### (Fol. 201 b, col. 2, l. 15 *ab ima*.)

Also the same year, on the nones of June[2], at Canterbury, St Thomas the martyr was translated—the fiftieth year after his martyrdom—by the aforesaid Archbishop Stephen of Canterbury. How this solemnity was performed ought to be known to all people, and I will endeavour to relate the manner of it briefly. Archbishop Stephen Langton, from the hour that he had received that dignity, after he had reached England, and the convent had returned from its banishment, bethought himself continually how he could honour the relics of his predecessor the glorious martyr St Thomas by translation, and made large provision of the things necessary against the time when it should be actually done. Then when he had given notice to the people throughout the country of the set day on which he would make the solemn translation, so many great personages came, and people as it were without number, that the city of Canterbury, and the suburbs, and the little towns around near adjoining thereto, were unable to receive in their houses all this people that came. King Henry III came also, at the request of the Archbishop of Canterbury. He stayed the eve and day of the translation

---

[1] Information about this Chronicle, which for many reasons deserves to be published in full, will be found in Stubbs's Preface to Vol. II. of the works of Gervase (Rolls Series). I am indebted for help in translating the French to Mr E. G. W. Braunholtz, Reader in the Romance Languages at Cambridge.

[2] A mistake for July.

with the archbishop, and together with him all the great men that were come, entirely at the archbishop's expense. Besides this, in the entrances of this city, at each gate, the archbishop caused the barrels of wine to be laid on their sides in bowers in the middle of the street, and his servants to be set there, to give liberally to the people during the heat without any payment of money. And also in four places within the city in the thoroughfares he caused the barrels to be set in the same manner to serve the common people. And in the four wine cellars he caused it to be forbidden to sell anything to the strange folk, but only [to give] entirely at his expense, and this by the service of his own people appointed for the purpose. For at that time these were the only places within the city where wine was to be found on sale.

Things outside being thus ordered, Archbishop Stephen and Walter the prior, together with all the convent of Christ Church, in the next night before the day of the translation, drew near to the sepulchre of the martyr in due form of devotion, and there at first they all applied themselves to their prayers as far as the shortness of the night might suffer them. Then were the stones of the tomb removed without injury by the hands of the monks appointed thereunto, and the others all rose up and drew near, and gazing upon the martyr they could not restrain their tears for joy. And then once more they all applied themselves to prayers in common, except certain monks who were specially chosen for their holy living to remove that precious treasure out of the sepulchre. These lifted him and put him in a seemly wooden chest adorned for the purpose, the which was well strengthened with iron, and they fastened it also carefully with iron nails, and then carried him to a seemly and secret place, until they should celebrate solemnly on the morrow the day of the translation.

Then in the morning all the prelates assembled themselves in the mother church, to wit the aforementioned Pandulf, legate of the holy church of Rome, and Stephen, Archbishop of Canterbury, with all the other bishops, his suffragans, who were come, save three, of whom one was dead, and two were excused by reason of sickness. These went forthwith to the place where the glorious martyr abode, in the presence of the aforesaid King of England, Henry III, and the prelates thereto appointed devoutly took the chest on their shoulders, and carried it into the choir before the altar of the Trinity which is to the east of the patriarchal chair. There they put him honourably with all reverence under another wooden chest very richly adorned with gold and precious stones. It was also covered all over with plate of gold and richly garnished.

Ausi memes cel an la none de Jun a Caunterbire fust seint Thomas le martir translaté, le an de sun martyrement l., per lerseueske Estephene avaunt nome de Canterbire. Coment ceste sollempnete estoyt feste a tote gent uoil estre conu, et me a forceray de cele la manere brevement parcunter. Lerseueske Estephene de Langetone del hure ke cele dignete out ressu, apres ceo ke en Engletere fust ariue et le couent del exil reuenu estoyt, se purpensa totes hures coment les reliqes sun predecessur Seint Thomas le glorious martyr poeyt honurer par la translatiun fere, et la purueaunce des choses nessessaires largement fist, cum ia mustre en fest serra. Dunt cum del iur certein ke cele translatiun sollempne fere uoloyt au puple parmye le tere out la notificatiun fest, tauns des grauns hi sunt venuz, et puple cum sauns numbre, ke la cite de Caunterbire, ne la suburbe, ne les menues uiles enuiroun a cele yoignauntes procheynes, le puple taunt uenu ne poeyent en lurs mesuns resceyure. Le roi ausi Henry le iij a la requeste lerseueske de Caunterbire uenu hi estoit. Si demora oue lerseueske et ansemble oue ly tuz les grauns ke venus estoyent la veile et le iur de la translatiun en tuz custages. Estre ceo, en les entrees de la cite a chescune porte en my la rue les toneaus de vin en foylis fist cocher lerseueske, et ces mynistres mettre pur largement au puple doner en la chalyne sauns paer accune moneye. E ausi en quatre lyus de diens la cite en les quarfoucs en memes la manere fist les toneaus mettre pur seruir a la mene gent, e defendre fist en les iiij celers de vin ke riens ny fust au puple estraunge uendu, si nun pleynement a ces custages, et ceo par seruice de ces gens a ceo assignes. Quar nestoyt lors de diens la cite en plus de lyut uin troue a uendre.

En teu manere les choses de hors ordines, lerseueske Estefene et Gauter le priur ansemble oue tut le couent del eglise Jhu Crist en la nuyt procheyne deuaunt le iur de la translatiun en due furme de deuociun au sepulcre del martyr approcherent. E ilukes au comencement en lurs orisuns se donerent tuz taunt cum la brefte de la nuyt le poeyt suffrir. Puys sunt les peres de la tumbe sauns blemysement remues per les meyns des moygnes a ceo ordines, et se leuerent les autres tuz si aprocherent et cel martyr de ioye regardauns ne se poeyent des lermes tenir. E puys autrefoyz as orisuns se unt dones tuz en comune hors pris accuns des moygnes ke de seinte vie especiaument elu furent a cel tresor precious hors de sepulcre remuer. Les queus le unt leue et en une chace de fust honeste a ceo appareylee le unt mys, la quele de fer bien yert asseurie si la fermerent queyntement par clous de fer, et puys en lyu honeste et priue le porterent taunt ke lendemeyn le iur de la translatiun sollempnement a celebrer.

Puys le matyn en cele mere eglise se assemblerent les prelats tuz, cest asauoyr, Pandulf auant nome de la seinte eglise de Rome legat, et Esteuene erseueske de Caunterbire, oue les autres eueskes ces suffragans tuz uenuz, hors pris troys, des queus lun mort estoyt, et les deus par maladie furent escuses. Ceus en la presence le Roy Dengletere auaunt nome Henry le iij au lyu ou le martyr glorious fust demore tost alerent, et la chace pristrent les prelats a ceo ordines sur lurs espaules, si la porterent deuoutement en quer deuaunt lauter de la Trinite ke est en le orient del see patriarchal. Ilukes de suz un autre chace de fust trerichement de oer et des peres preciouses appareylee en tote reuerence honurablement cele mistrent. Si demurt par plate de oer tote part couerte et richement garnye.

### (2) *Appendix ad Quadrilogum.*

(*Materials*, Vol. IV. p. 426.)

In the fiftieth year of the passion of the glorious martyr Thomas, Archbishop of Canterbury, the venerable father Stephen, his fourth successor, and the convent of the church of Canterbury, being anxious to translate the body of the precious martyr, prepared with much care all that they deemed necessary for such a solemnity. After appropriate

fastings and prayers, the archbishop, and Richard, Bishop
of Salisbury, and the convent, on the twenty-seventh of
June, in the beginning of the night, assembled, as they
had determined, in the crypt where the body of the blessed
martyr lay; and after they had spent some time in prayer,
they caused the marble stone, which covered the martyr's
tomb, to be removed. So under the eyes of all present, that
sometime instrument of the Holy Ghost was found, in his
sacerdotal vestments, which were partly perished with age,
and the other insignia appropriate to the burial of a chief
priest[1].

While all wept for joy, and prayed, certain specially appointed monks, taking the precious body in their hands,
delivered it to the archbishop to be laid in a coffin. While
the rest applied themselves to the prayers which had been
begun, the archbishop took the body from the aforesaid
monks, and placed it with his own hands in the feretrum,
all but a few small bones, which he kept out of the coffin,
to distribute to great men and churches in honour of the
martyr himself. When the body had been duly arranged
by the hands of the archbishop, the coffin was very firmly
fastened with iron nails, and carried by the hands of monks
to a bier in an honourable place, and there kept secretly
till the day for the solemn translation[2].

As the day of translation approached, an innumerable

---

[1] Lapidem marmoreum, quo sepulcrum martyris tegebatur,
amoveri fecerunt. Omnibus itaque qui aderant intuentibus, inventum
est illud organum quondam Spiritus Sancti in vestibus sacerdotalibus,
licet ex vetustate pro parte consumptis, et caeteris insignibus quae
summi sacerdotis decuerant sepulturam.

[2] Monachi ad hoc deputati corpus pretiosum manibus assumentes
archiepiscopo in capsa reponendum tradiderunt. Caeteris itaque
coeptis orationibus insistentibus, archiepiscopus a praedictis fratribus
corpus accipiens totum in feretro suis manibus collocavit, exceptis
paucis ossiculis, quae extra capsam retinuit, magnis viris et ecclesiis
ad ipsius martyris honorem distribuenda. Corpore siquidem per
manus archiepiscopi decenter disposito, capsa firmissime clavis
ferreis obseratur, et manibus monachorum ad locum honestum et
feretrum deportata usque ad diem translationis solenniter faciendae
secretius est conservata.

concourse of people poured into Canterbury, to do the martyr the honour which he deserved and obtain his aid in their necessities. Those who took part in the solemnity included the venerable father Pandulf, legate of the apostolic see, Stephen, Archbishop of Canterbury, William, Archbishop of Rheims, Henry, King of England, with his counts and nobles, bishops, abbots, and priors, and ecclesiastics of different countries....Such a number of people poured in to this festival, that the city of Canterbury and the neighbouring towns and the district round could scarcely take the multitude in.

At nine o'clock on the seventh of July, the king, the archbishop, the bishops, abbots, princes, and magnates, who had come together, bore the treasure from the crypt, where it had been laid, to the altar of the holy martyr, and in the sight of the people they laid it in the place prepared for the purpose; and sealing it securely there, they passed the remainder of the day in the praises of the martyr and gladness of heart in the Lord.

It has seemed hardly necessary to reprint the Icelandic original of the next piece. The translation here given is Mr Magnússon's, with corrections in notes where required.

### (3) *Thómas Saga Erkibyskups.*

(Rolls Series, ed. Magnússon, Vol. II. p. 197.)

When one thousand two hundred and twenty-four years[1] had passed from the birth of our Lord Jesus Christ, in the fiftieth year after the passion of the holy Thomas, in the days of Pope Honorius, the third of that name, who sat the eighth in the apostolic see after Pope Alexander the third, and in the days of Stephen, Archbishop of Canterbury, who was the fourth after the worthy Thomas who held rule in that see, the love and miracles of the holy Thomas so enkindled the hearts of the English people, that by the

[1] This computation of course goes on the assumption that "the account called Anno Domini" is four years out.

consent and the agreement of the lord pope they will endure
no longer that their most glorious father shall lie so low in
the crypt as when first he was entombed, but rather desire
that he be honoured and raised into a worthy place, in
order that all folk may bow to him and become partakers
of[1] his merits....

[Here follow the praises of Archbishop Stephen.]

It therefore accordeth well with his goodness of soul in
other things that he should call unto Canterbury certain
worthy teachers, quietly though that matter went at first.
Of these may be mentioned Richard, the Bishop of Salisbury. Lord Archbishop Stephen also commandeth all
canons, monks, and all the learned men there assembled,
to fast amid holy prayers for the next three days before
going down to the resting place of God's martyr. And when
the chest had been made in a fair fashion with a trusty lock
to it, the lord archbishop goeth down into the crypt together
with the learned men some time after compline, when the
world's people were already at rest. This took place on the
fifth of the calends of July, two nights, to wit, before the
mass[2] of the apostles Peter and Paul. They now proceed
all together in such due humility unto the stone vault[3],
that they prostrate themselves to earth in tearful prayers
around the tomb. Having prayed a long time and devoutly,
the archbishop ordereth certain of the monks to remove the
marble slab which closed the stone vault[3]. And having
done this, they find the fair treasure and fragrant organ of
the Holy Ghost shrouded in such raiment as appertaineth
to the highest teacher, which, however, fell into dust by
reason of its great eld when it was touched. The devotion
of those present while performing this work was borne out
by their flowing tears. The same brothers who had laid
open the grave, took up the most holy bones, laying them
down again on a certain costly cloth. And this having been
done with every care, they bring the holy relic before the

---

[1] Rather, "be helped by."
[2] Literally, "the day of the return home."
[3] The word "þro," a tomb, contains no suggestion of a *vault*.

archbishop himself. Then the chest is brought forward, for the archbishop chooseth for himself the service of laying the bones into the chest, which was done in such a way, that a white weed was laid under and above. But whilst he ministereth at this blessed service, the learned men lie kneeling around in prayers and tears. A small portion of the bones the archbishop leaveth outside the chest, in order to divide them among certain glorious cathedral churches, or to make a loving present of them unto certain excellent persons, in order that the memory of God's dearly beloved one may spread the more, the more widely his holy relics shall be worshipped. All this having been fairly fulfilled, and the chest having been closed, the archbishop enjoineth the same brothers to carry it away unto a certain honourable yet hidden place, for in this affair he acteth on the forethought that the solemn translation of Thomas shall take place then first, when news hath had time to go abroad throughout the land, that the greatest lords both from the church and from the pope's[1] court may be present at such a blessed service. For this reason he fixeth an interval of ten days, ordering that on the last day of the nones of the month of July[2] they shall all come to Canterbury, learned men as well as unlearned, who have a mind to worship the holy archbishop Thomas.

Concerning this the master[3] relateth, that he may not state the number of the multitudes of people who assembled on the settled day at Canterbury, as the city of Canterbury and all surrounding villages were so filled with people that many had to abide under tents or under the open sky. These two lords were there, the worthy father and legate of the holy[4] see, Fandulfhus by name, and the Archbishop of Reims. None, beside these, knew we to mention, as

---

[1] Magnússon is evidently wrong in inserting the word "pope's," *Kurie* must mean "the court," i.e. the king's court.

[2] July 7, not as printed in Magnússon July 1st.

[3] It is not known who is intended, but the narrative is evidently connected with the foregoing from the *Quadrilogus*.

[4] *Postuligs* = "apostolic," not "holy," as M.

having come from abroad; but among those from England itself we may name first King Henry, the son[1] of Henry, who was there surrounded by earls, barons, and every kind of mighty folk, therewithal bishops, abbots, priors, and the other orders of learned men from various districts. Now, in God's name, cometh the third hour of the nonae of July, at which hour the bishop standeth robed together with the other bishops and orders of learned men aforenamed, who then proceed amidst solemn singing down into the crypt, where the chest was kept. The solemnity with which it was brought thence up into the church, and was placed [on high[2]] over the altar, where preparations had been made for it, may be best told in these few words, that the church of Canterbury showed forth in a free manner every honour which she could do unto her father, in bells rung, in song, and splendid appointments, not only inside the church, but also in the joyance in which the city manifested its solemn hilarity, the king and all other folk deeming themselves as partakers of a divine gift if they might in any way minister to the festivity.

(p. 211) The next thing done by lord Stephen, Archbishop of Canterbury, was that, in his devotion he resolved to convert the offerings made to the holy Thomas into a shrine for him. And when this had been settled by the urging of the king and other mighty folk in the land, the archbishop procureth for the work the greatest master in the craft who could be found within those lands. But when the commonalty of England got full certainty of this, the love which the people bore to St Thomas was soon revealed, since they would hear of his shrine being made of no other metal but gold alone, which indeed had to be done. Hence the pilgrims to St Thomas's shrine repeat the saw of the English, that after that time England never grew so wealthy in gold as before, and for that they give thanks unto God. Now by this mighty expense and choice workmanship the shrine was the most excellent work of art that had ever

[1] I.e. grandson.
[2] M. leaves these words (í hæð) untranslated.

been seen, being set all round with stones, wherever beauty and effect might thereby be best set off. When the shrine was finished the archbishop depositeth therewithin the holy relics of the worthy martyr, Archbishop[1] Thomas, and placeth it above the middle of the high altar, only so high that it rested on the upper table thereof[2], one face of it pointing to the east, the other to the west.

### (4) *Matthew Paris, Hist. Ang.*

(Rolls Series, Vol. II. p. 241.)

And at the same season the body of the blessed Thomas, Archbishop of Canterbury and martyr, was raised out of its marble sarcophagus in the crypt of the church of Canterbury by the Archbishop of Canterbury, Stephen, of glorious memory, who thought that it was an undignified position for him to lie as it were in the basement of the church and in stone. He had prepared for the honourable reception of the body a shrine of the purest gold of Ophir and precious stones, and of workmanship even costlier than the material[3]. The translation took place the day after the octave of the apostles Peter and Paul, which was the anniversary of King Henry II, under whom the martyr suffered, in the presence of King Henry III, and a great number of archbishops, bishops, abbots, priors, and magnates innumerable, both from beyond the seas and from this side:—in the presence moreover of the incomparable artists, Master Walter of Colchester, sacrist of St Albans, and Master Elias of Dereham[4], canon of Salisbury, by

---

[1] This word is not in the original, as printed by M.

[2] Minute as this description is, it is not borne out by any other authority, and is due to some misunderstanding. The shrine had an altar of its own.

[3] Praeparaverat autem thecam ad corpus honorifice collocandum de auro obrizo purissimo et gemmis pretiosissimis, artificio materiam superante.

[4] The accounts of the convent contain a good many payments to Elias of Dereham.

whose skilled advice all the necessary preparations both for the making of the shrine and for the actual raising and translation were carried out without a hitch[1]. Nor was there ever seen on earth a translation so largely attended and so magnificent, where so many honoured personages of different nations took part. For all thought it proper to honour in common Christ's holy martyr, who did not fear to shed his blood for the universal church, and was in no wise afraid to stand for its freedom to the death.

A few samples of monastic Annals may be of interest.

### (5) *Annals of Waverley.*

(Rolls Series, p. 293.)

This year, on the nones of July, the body of the glorious martyr Thomas, Archbishop of Canterbury, was translated by the revered Stephen, archbishop of that see, in the fiftieth year of his passion, from the crypt of the church, where he had lain for nearly fifty years, to a more exalted position, behind the high altar of the church, and placed in a coffin wonderfully wrought of gold and silver, and marvellously adorned with precious gems. To this translation so vast an assemblage of men and women came together from various parts of the world, that it is said that never had such a multitude of people been brought together in one spot in England in all previous ages. For an edict had gone forth from the archbishop, and had been published in divers kingdoms and countries, nearly two years before, with regard to the translation; and the lord archbishop himself, throughout his manors and estates, to the utmost extent of his means, had ordered with wonderful largesse and lavish generosity preparation to be made for men and animals, and to be offered to all comers both in

[1] Praesentibus etiam incomparabilibus artificibus, magistris Waltero de Colecestria, sacrista de Sancto Albano, et Elia de Derham, canonico Saresbiriensi, quorum consiliis et ingeniis omnia quae ad artificium thecae et ipsius elevationis et translationis necessaria fuerant, irreprehensibiliter parabantur.

Canterbury and in the neighbourhood. And although the preparation was not sufficient for all and each, yet it showed his goodwill, because he had aimed at providing necessaries for all.

### (6) *Annals of Dunstable.*

(Rolls Series, p. 58.)

The same year, the day after the octave of Peter and Paul, the body of the blessed Thomas the martyr was solemnly translated, in the fiftieth year from his passion, which was to us all a jubilee. Four and twenty archbishops and bishops, English and foreign, took part in it. On that day the Archbishop of Reims celebrated the high mass. On the day before, he dedicated the altar before the shrine in honour of the blessed martyr. The Archbishop of Canterbury had proclaimed an indulgence of two years of penance, extended over the ensuing fortnight to all comers. The feasting, in food and drink, in vessels of gold and silver, and costly draperies, was such that we do not read of the like being held since the time of King Ahasuerus. Besides this, we must not omit to mention that the archbishop built a palace suitable for such a feast, the like of which has not been seen, we believe, since the time of Solomon[1].

### (7) *Higden, Polychronicon.*

(Trevisa's translation, Rolls Series, Vol. iii. p. 200.)

Also this yere seint Thomas of Caunturbury the marter was translated by Stevene the archebisshop of Caunterbury. Durynge the solempnite he fonde hey and provendre to alle men that wolde axe it, in the wey bitwene Londoun and Caunturbury. Also in the day of the translacioun he made wyne to renne in pipes continualliche in divers places of the citee. And so the coste that Stevene made in this

---

[1] Tanto convivio dictus archiepiscopus condignum palatium construxit, quale visum non credimus a tempore Salomonis.

solempnite his fourthe successour Bonefacius paide it unnethe.

Hoc etiam anno facta est translatio beati Thomae martyris per Stephanum archiepiscopum, qui durante solemnitate exhibuit cuicumque petenti fenum et praebendam a Londoniis usque Cantuariam per viam itineranti; fecit etiam per totam diem translationis vinum jugiter in canalibus per varia urbis loca distillare: unde et expensas quas Stephanus in hac solemnitate exhibuit quartus ejus successor Bonéfacius vix persolvit.

## (8) *Robert of Gloucester*.

(*Life and Martyrdom of Thomas Becket* by Robert of Gloucester, ed. W. H. Black, Percy Society, 1845, p. 124.)

Therfori to honurye this holi bodi: ther com folc ynough,
Of bischops and of abbotes: menion[1] thider drough;
Of priours and of persones: and of meni other clerkes also,
Of eorles and of barouns: and of meni knyghtes therto;
Of serjants and of squiers: and of hosebondes ynowe,
And of simple men ek of the lond.: so thicke thider drowe,
That al the lond theraboute: the contrayes wide and longe,
Might unethe al that folc: that ther com, afonge[2].
So that this heghe men: that sholde this dede do,
Were in care hou hi[3] mighte: for presse come therto;
So that the Archebischop Stevene: of wham that ich you
     er sede,
And the Bischop Richard of Salisbure: nome[4] hem to rede[5];
And the Priour, Water, of the hous: and the Covent also,
Wenden hem alle in priveite: this dede forto do.
Binyghte as the men leye and slepe: and lute[6] thereof
     thoghte,
Hi nome up this holi bones: and in a chiste hem broghte.
And sette hem up in a privei stede: forte[7] the dai were
     icome,
That was icrid[8] into al that lond: that he scholde beo up
     ynome.

| | | |
|---|---|---|
| [1] Many one. | [2] Take in. | [3] They. |
| [4] Took. | [5] Counsel. | [6] Little. |
| [7] Until. | [8] Cried, proclaimed. | |

This was in the month of Jul: right evene the sovethe dai,
That bi a Tywesdai was tho: as al that folc isay.
Tho[1] this dai was icome: to this mynstre wende anon
The Kyng Henri the yunge child: and this heghe men
    echon[2].
Aboute underne of the dai: to this holi bodi hi come;
Pandolf wente furste therto: the Legat of Rome;
And the Archebischop of Canterbury: and of Reyns also,
That for the silve[3] thinge come: fram biyunde see therto.
And Sire Huberd de Brom[4]: that was the heghe Justise,
And four grete louerdlings that were: noble men and wise,
Upe here schuldren hi nome: this holi bodi anon;
And the bischops and abbotes: were ek meni on.
To the hegh [auter] of the Trinite: this holi bones hi bere,
And leide the chiste al therwith: in a noble schryne there.
This King Henri was so young: that he ne therste[5] noght,
With othere bere this holi bones: leste me[6] hurte him oght.
This was bi a Tywesdai: that this bones up hi nome:
All his cheances that he hadde: by Tywesdai hi come[7].

### C. THE SHRINE AND THE HEAD.

The next documents to be considered are those which
show us what relics of St Thomas were exhibited to pilgrims who visited Canterbury. We are fortunate enough
to possess a double record of the visit of a Bohemian am-

---

[1] Then, when.      [2] Each one.      [3] Self-same.
[4] De Burgh.        [5] Durst.         [6] May.
[7] A sermon of Archbishop Langton's has been preserved—preached,
it seems, on some anniversary of the translation—but it contains
no facts but these:
"Those who translated the martyr designed that it should be done
on a Tuesday, because he suffered on a Tuesday....But we testify in
Christ that it was by no human forethought, but by God's gracious
disposal of events, that it was in the fiftieth year of his passion that
his venerable body received the honour of translation....It is another
remarkable fact, which the providence of God designed for the glory
of the martyr, that the martyr was translated on the very day on which
King Henry, in whose days he suffered, was laid in the ground."
                    (In Giles, *Vita S. Thomae*, Vol. II. p. 292.)

bassador, Leo of Rotzmital, in 1446. Stanley gives extracts from these records in the Appendix to his *Memorials*, referring for a fuller description to an article in the *Quarterly Review* for March, 1852. One of the two records, by a man named Schassek, is in Latin, the other by his companion, Tetzel, is in German.

### (1) *Schassek.*

In this church Saint Thomas was killed....During evensong, by wicked men, who desired to gratify an ungodly king, he had his head cut off, calling upon God and the saints. We saw there his sepulchre and his head. The sepulchre is composed of pure gold, and adorned with jewels, and is enriched with such magnificent gifts that I know nothing like it....There we were shown all the relics: first the head of St Thomas the archbishop, and the shaven or bald part of the same; then a pillar in front of the chapel of the Mother of God, by which he used to pray and to enjoy conversation with the Blessed Virgin....There is a spring in the convent, the waters of which had five times turned into blood, and once into milk....I made a note of all the rest of the sacred relics which we inspected there. They were these:—we saw a girdle of the Blessed Virgin, a shred of the coat of Christ, and three thorns of His crown. Then we gazed on the shirt of St Thomas, and his brain, and some blood of the apostles St Thomas and St John. We beheld also the sword with which St Thomas of Canterbury was beheaded, and some hairs of the Mother of God, and part of her sepulchre....And many other things were shown us, of which I have made no note here.

In eo templo occisus est divus Thomas....Sub vespertinis precibus a nefariis hominibus, qui regi impio gratificari cupiebant, Deum et sanctos invocans, capite truncatus est. Ibi vidimus sepulchrum et caput ipsius. Sepulchrum ex puro auro conflatum est, et gemmis adornatum, tamque magnificis donariis ditatum, ut par ei nesciam....Ibi omnes reliquiae nobis monstratae sunt: primum caput divi Thomae archiepiscopi, rasuraque vel calvities ejusdem; deinde columna ante sacellum

Genitricis Dei, juxta quam orare et colloquio Beatae Virginis...
perfrui solitus est....Fons est in eo coenobio, cujus aquae quinquies in sanguinem et semel in lac commutatae fuerant...Cae-
teras sacras reliquias, quas ibi conspeximus, omnes annotavi,
quae hae sunt: primum vidimus redimiculum Beatae Virginis,
frustum de veste Christi, tresque spinas de corona ejusdem.
Deinde contemplati sumus sancti Thomae subuculum (*sic*), et
cerebrum ejus, et divorum Thomae Johannisque apostolorum
sanguinem. Spectavimus etiam gladium, quo decollatus est
sanctus Thomas Cantuariensis, et crines Matris Dei, et portionem de sepulchro ejusdem....Et alia plurima nobis monstra-
bantur, quae hoc loco a me annotata non sunt.

(2)  *Tetzel of Nuremberg.*

(Stanley, *ibidem.*)

The shrine that St Thomas lies in, the poorest thing
about it is gold; and it is long and broad, so that a middle-
sized person could lie in it; but it is adorned with pearls
and precious stones in so costly a fashion that they say
there is no costlier shrine in christendom, and also no such
great miracles are done as there....And under the shrine is
the place where the dear lord St Thomas was beheaded, and
over the shrine aloft a coarse hair shirt that he wore; and
on the left-hand side as you go in, there is a spring, of
which St Thomas used to drink every day. At St Thomas's
tide it has five times turned into milk and blood. My lord
Herr Leo drank of it, and all his servants. And after that,
they go into a little vault like a chapel, where St Thomas
was martyred. There they showed us the sword with
which his head was cut off. There they exhibit also a
notable piece of the holy Cross, also one of the nails, and
the right arm of the dear lord the Knight St George, and
in a monstrance certain thorns of the crown of thorns.
Out of the chapel they go to a stone chair, where is the
figure of our Lady, which often talked with St Thomas.
The said figure now stands in the choir, and wears a crown
of right costly stones and pearls, which is valued at a great
price.

Der sarch, darinne sant Thomas leit, ist das geringst daran gold, und ist lang und weit, das ein mitlein person darin ligen mag; aber mit perlein und edelgestein so ist er gar seer kostlich geziert, das man meint, das kein kostlicher sarch sey in der christenheit, und da auch so gross wunderzeichen geschehen als da....Und unter dem sarch ist die stat, do der lieb herr sant Thomas enthaubtet worden ist, und ob dem sarch hecht ein grob hären hemd, das er angetragen hatt, und auf der linken seiten, so man hinein geet, do ist einn brunn, darauss hat sant Thomas altag trunken. Der hat sich zu sant Thomas zeiten funfmal verwandelt in milch und blut. Darauss trank meinn herr Herr Lew und all sein diener. Und darnach geet man in ein kleine grufft als in ein cappellen, da man sant Thomas gemartert hat. Da zeiget man uns das schwert, damit man jm den kopf abgeschlagen hat. Da weiset man auch ein merklich stuck des heiligen creuzes, auch der nägel einen und den rechten arm des lieben herrn Ritter sant Görgen und etlich dorn in einer mostranzen von der dürnen kron. Auss der cappellen get man heifur zu einem steinen stul, da ist unser Frawen bild, das gar oft mit sant Thomas geredet hat. Das selbig stet iezunt im kor und hat ser von kostlichen gesteen und perlein ein kron auf, die man umb gross gut schätzt.

The third record of a pilgrimage to Canterbury is not only from the hand of a greater man, but shows a far greater power of observation. Erasmus's description is in fact a guide book to the cathedral with scarcely a mistake in it. We can follow the pilgrim round, see what he saw at each spot, and in what order the items were shown to him[1]. His visit took place in 1512, or the year before or after. Erasmus was accompanied by the great Colet.

### (3) *Erasmus, Peregrinatio Religionis ergo.*

*Menedemus.* Did you fail to visit Thomas, Archbishop of Canterbury?

*Ogygius.* Certainly not. There was never a more devout pilgrimage.

---

[1] The *Peregrinatio* has been translated, and furnished with a copious and erudite commentary, by the antiquary John Gough Nichols. The following translation is independently made.

*Me.* I should like to hear about it, if it is not troubling you.

*Og.* On the contrary; do me the favour to let me tell you. Kent is the name of that part of England which looks across to France and Flanders. The capital of it is Canterbury. There are two monasteries in it, almost touching one another,—both Benedictine. The one which bears the title of St Augustine's appears to be the more ancient; the one now called St Thomas's seems to have been the seat of the archbishop, where he lived with a few chosen monks; just as nowadays bishops have their houses adjoining the church, but separate from those of the other canons. In former days both the bishops and the canons were monks[1]. There are evident traces that prove it. The church dedicated to St Thomas[2] rises so majestically into the sky as to inspire devotion even when seen far off. So now, with its splendour, it obstructs the light of its neighbour, and throws into the shade the place which in old days was the most religious. There are two immense towers[3], which seem to greet the traveller far off, and which fill the neighbouring country far and wide with the wonderful booming of the bronze bells. In the south porch of the church stand the stone figures of three armed men whose ungodly hands slaughtered the saint. Their family names are inscribed below,—Tuscus, Fuscus, and Berrus[4].

*Me.* Why is such an honour bestowed on such ungodly men?

*Og.* It is the same honour that is bestowed on Judas, Pilate, Caiaphas, and the band of wicked soldiers, whom you see artistically carved on gilded altars. The names are added in order that nobody hereafter may assume them as

---

[1] With this view of history we are not now concerned.

[2] The dedication of Christ Church has never been officially changed. Popularly Erasmus might be justified. See p. 141.

[3] Stanley remarks that the N.W. tower did not stand so high.

[4] Stanley attempts an explanation of these names, but the probability is that Erasmus was not interested in them, and set them down out of his own head. Hentzner, to whom Stanley refers, seems to have written with his Erasmus before him.

titles of honour. They are offered to the eye, in order that no courtier hereafter may lay hands either upon bishops or upon the possessions of the church. For those three officers went mad with what they had done, and did not recover their reason until they implored the favour of St Thomas.

*Me.* What unfailing compassion the martyrs show!

*Og.* As you enter, the spacious dignity of the building opens out. Into this part of it anybody may go.

*Me.* Is there nothing to see there?

*Og.* Nothing but the vastness of the fabric, and a few books fastened to the pillars—among them the Gospel of Nicodemus—and somebody's grave[1].

*Me.* What next?

*Og.* Iron grates[2] bar your way, but allow you to look, into the space between the end of the church[3] and the choir. This is reached up a great number of steps, under which a vaulted passage leads into the north transept. There they show you a wooden altar dedicated to the Blessed Virgin; it is very small, and in no way remarkable, except as a monument of antiquity, which puts to shame our modern luxuriousness[4]. There the saintly man is said to have paid his last salutation to the Virgin, when death was close at hand. At the altar is the point of the sword which cut off the top of the good bishop's head, and mixed up his brains, to hasten his death. We kissed devoutly the sacred rust on the iron, for love of the martyr. Here we turned aside and went down into the crypt chapel, which has its own guides and exponents. There in the first place is exhibited the pierced skull of the martyr. The rest is covered with

[1] Abp. Whittlesea's. Stanley calls it a "shrine." (p. 247), perhaps by mistake for Winchelsea's, which was in the S.E. transept.

[2] These grates formed a screen behind the altar of the Holy Cross under the western arch of the central tower.

[3] Erasmus speaks of the nave as if it were a separate *aedes*.

[4] Erasmus is our only authority for the dedication of this altar to the B. V. M. He may perhaps have confused it with that of the Lady Chapel close by, which superseded the chapel of St Benet.

silver, but the top of the cranium is bare for people to kiss[1]. At the same time they show you a plate of lead, inscribed with the name of Thomas of Acre. There in the dark hang the under-garments, waistbands, and breeches of haircloth, with which the bishop subdued his flesh, the very sight of which strikes you with horror, and puts to shame our softness and our comforts.

*Me.* And possibly those of the monks themselves.

*Og.* Of that I am not in a position to say yes or no; it is no business of mine.

*Me.* Very true.

*Og.* Now we go back to the choir. The lockers on the north side are opened. It is astonishing what a quantity of bones are brought out of them—skulls, jaws, teeth, hands, fingers, whole arms. We kissed them all in worship, and there would have been no end to it, if my companion in that pilgrimage, who did not at all like the business, had not stopped the showman's enthusiasm.

*Me.* Who was your companion?

*Og.* An Englishman named Gratianus Pullus[2], a learned and godly man, but with less sympathy than I should have liked for this side of religion.

*Me.* A Wicliffite, I suppose.

*Og.* I do not think so, although he had read Wiclif's works. I do not know where he got them.

*Me.* Did he hurt the feelings of the expositor?

*Og.* An arm was produced, with flesh upon it still raw. He shrank from kissing it, and his face showed something of his distaste. The expositor quickly shut his wares up again. After that we beheld the reredos and adornments of the altar, and then the things kept under the altar—all very rich. You would say that Midas and Croesus were beggars, if you saw such a quantity of gold and silver.

*Me.* No kissing there?

---

[1] Illic primum exhibetur calvaria martyris perforata; reliqua tecta sunt argento, summa cranii pars nuda patet osculo.

[2] I.e. Colet, Dean of St Paul's.

*Og.* No; it was a different class of desires which passed over my mind.

*Me.* What was that?

*Og.* I thought with a sigh that I had no relics of that kind at home.

*Me.* What a sacrilegious desire!

*Og.* I confess it; and before leaving the church I begged the saint's pardon on bended knees. After that, we were conducted into the treasury. Good God! what a display of silk vestments there was there, and what a quantity of golden candlesticks! There too we saw the pastoral staff of St Thomas. It looked like a cane plated with silver; scarcely any weight; no workmanship; and not higher than your waist.

*Me.* No cross[1]?

*Og.* Not that I saw. A cloak was shown, made of silk, but of coarse thread, and without any ornament of gold or gems. A handkerchief was to be seen there, too, still bearing the stains of sweat from his neck, and those of his blood, very plain. These specimens of the simplicity of old times we kissed with pleasure.

*Me.* Are these things not shown to everybody?

*Og.* Certainly not.

*Me.* How came they to trust you so much as to hide nothing from you?

*Og.* I had some acquaintance with the Most Reverend the Archbishop, William Warham: he gave me a word or two of introduction.

*Me.* I hear from many quarters, a man of great kindness.

*Og.* Kindness itself you would say, if you only knew—and so learned, so high principled, so devout, that there is no endowment of a perfect bishop that you would fail to find in him. Well, we were led from these objects to the upper regions. For behind the high altar you go up again into what is like a new church. There in a chapel is shown

---

[1] No doubt he means the archiepiscopal cross.

the whole of the good man's countenance gilded over and embellished with many jewels[1]. Here an unexpected occurrence almost brought our whole pleasure to a sad end.

*Me.* I wonder what the disaster was.

*Og.* Here my companion Gratianus disgraced himself. After a moment's prayer, he put this question to the interpreter who sat there, "Pray, good father," he said, "is it true, as I have been told, that Thomas in his lifetime was very kind to the poor?" "Certainly," he answered, and began to tell many stories of his goodness to those who were badly off. Then Gratianus said, "I suppose that that disposition of his is not changed unless for the better." The interpreter agreed. He began again, "As the saint was so generous to the needy when he was himself poor and needed the aid of money for the requirements of a frail body, do you not think that now, when he is in such affluence, and has need of nothing, he would be little concerned, supposing some poor woman, with hungry children at home,...were to ask for pardon and then abstract some little part of all this wealth for the support of her family, as a gift or loan from a willing friend?" As the guardian of the golden head[2] made no reply, the vehement Gratianus said, "I am quite sure that the saint would be really pleased to relieve the wants of the poor with his riches, after death as before." Then the mystagogue began to frown and pout and look at us with the eyes of a Gorgon; and I have no doubt that if he had not known that we were introduced by the archbishop, he would have ejected us from the church, spitting upon us and reviling us. For my part, I appeased the man's wrath as best I could with smooth words, saying that Gratianus did not mean what he said, but was making one of his jokes, and at the same time I put down a shilling or two.

---

[1] Ab his igitur deducimur ad superiora. Nam post altare summum rursus velut in novum templum ascenditur. Illic in sacello quodam ostenditur tota facies optimi viri inaurata, multisque gemmis insignita.

[2] Assessor capitis aurei.

*Me.* I approve heartily of your piety....Now let me hear the dénoument of the tragedy.

*Og.* You shall; I will tell you quickly. At this point appeared the high mystagogue of all.

*Me.* Who was that? the abbot?

*Og.* He wears the mitre, and has the revenues of an abbot, only they do not call him so; he is called the prior, because the archbishop occupies the place of the abbot. Anciently whoever had the archiepiscopal jurisdiction there was always a monk.

*Me.* I should not mind if they called me the camel, if the revenues were fit for an abbot.

*Og.* I thought he seemed a man of piety and prudence combined, and well read in the divinity of Scotus. He opened for us the receptacle, in which the rest of the saint's body is said to repose[1].

*Me.* You saw his bones?

*Og.* No, that is not allowed; indeed, you could not do it without bringing a ladder; but the wooden receptacle encloses a golden one, and when it is drawn up by a pulley, it displays wealth beyond valuation[2].

*Me.* What does it consist of?

*Og.* The least valuable part of it was gold. Everything shone, and sparkled, and flashed with rare jewels of extraordinary size. Some were bigger than a goose's egg. There a number of the monks stood round with deep reverence: when the cover was removed, we all worshipped. The prior showed the jewels one after another, touching them with a white wand, and adding the French name,

[1] It is not certain who this prior was. If the pilgrimage took place, as Nichols thought, in the year 1518 or so (Colet died in 1519), then it was Thomas Goldwell, the last of the priors. But Erasmus does not seem to have returned to England about that time. He was in England from August 1511 to July 1514. During that period Thomas Goldstone II was prior.

[2] Is nobis aperuit thecam, in qua reliquum sancti viri corpus quiescere dicitur. ME. Vidisti ossa? OG. Id quidem fas non est; nec liceret, nisi admotis scalis: sed auream thecam theca contegit lignea: ea funibus sublata opes nudat inaestimabiles.

and what it was worth, and who gave it. For the principal ones were presents from crowned heads[1].

*Me.* The prior must have had a splendid memory.

*Og.* You are quite right—though practice makes it easier. He often does it. From this spot he took us back to the crypt. There the Virgin Mother has a dwelling place, though a dark one, where she is fenced round once and again with iron grates.

*Me.* What is she afraid of?

*Og.* Only thieves, I think. I never saw anything so loaded with jewels.

*Me.* Blind wealth, according to your account.

*Og.* When they brought lights, we saw a more than royal sight.

*Me.* Is she richer than the one at Walsingham?

*Og.* What she displays beats the other by a long way. What she keeps hidden I leave her to say. This one is only shown to great people or to special friends. Finally we were taken back to the treasury, where a case covered with black leather was fetched down and deposited on a table. It was opened, and in a moment we all fell on our knees and worshipped.

*Me.* What did it contain?

*Og.* Some ragged scraps of linen, most of them still showing signs of having been used for handkerchiefs. They told us that the saint employed them to wipe the sweat from his face or neck, the running of his nose, and things of that sort, incidental to the human frame. Then again dear Gratianus fell into disgrace. He was an Englishman, a well-known personage, and a great authority; and the prior kindly offered to present him with one of the linen rags, thinking that he could not offer anything more acceptable. But Gratianus, graceless in this instance, fingered one of them with signs of repulsion, laid it con-

---

[1] Ibi multa cum veneratione circumstabant aliquot monachi: sublato tegumento adoravimus omnes. Prior candida virga demonstrabat contactu singulas gemmas, addens nomen Gallicum, pretium et auctorem doni. Nam praecipuas monarchae dono miserant.

temptuously down, putting out his lips, as if pretending to whistle[1]. That was his habit when something happened that he disliked but thought contemptible. My mind was distracted between shame and fear. The prior, however, like a dull man, pretended not to see; he offered us a cup of wine, and sent us kindly away....On the way towards London, not long after you leave Canterbury, you come to a road which is very steep, and narrow too, and has, besides, such a precipitous bank on either side, that you cannot get out of the way; and you have no choice of roads, either. On the left-hand side is a begging-place for a number of old men[2]. One of them runs forward, directly they hear anybody on horseback coming. He sprinkles him with holy water, and then offers him the upper part of a shoe, with a brass ring round it, in which a piece of glass[3] is set, like a jewel. People kiss it and give a small coin.

*Me.* In a place like that I would rather find a begging-place for old men than a band of sturdy robbers.

*Og.* Gratianus was riding on my left, nearest to the begging-place. He was sprinkled with the water, but took it pretty well. When the shoe was offered, he asked what it meant. The man said it was St Thomas's shoe. My friend got angry, and turning to me, he said, "What do these cattle mean by making us kiss all good men's shoes?" ...I was sorry for the poor old man, and comforted his disappointment by giving him a little coin.

### (4) *Madame de Montreuil.*

(*State Papers* (1831), p. 583.)

The last recorded pilgrimage to the great shrine was that of Madame de Montreuil, of which Stanley has given a graphic description. On September 1 of the year 1538 Sir

---

[1] Or perhaps, "to give it a smacking kiss."

[2] This is of course the Hospital of St Nicholas at Harbledown.

[3] Probably the piece of rock crystal now set in a mazer, and preserved there.

William Penison wrote the following letter to Cromwell, a week before the demolition of the shrine began.

Right honnourable and my singulier good Lord, as louly as I can, I recommend me unto Your Lordeship. Please it the same to be adcertayned, that, ensuyng myne other letters, my Lady of Montreuill hath kept her journeys; so that upon Fryday last, at 6 of the cloc, she, accompayned with her gentilwomen and thambassadour of Fraunce, arryved in this towne; and the Maister of the Roles[1], with a good nombre of men, wheynt to myte her half a myle owt of the towne, where the Mayre and the Shryffes met with her, in saluting and welcomyng her in theyr best wyse, and so accompanyed, she was brought to her lodging, which she dyd like very well. Upon her said arryvall, the Lorde Priour[2] did present her fish of soundry sortes, wynes, and fruyttes, plentye; the Maister of the Roles dyd present her torches, and perchers of wax, a good nombre; fysshes of soundry sortes, wynes, and fruytes, plentye; the Mayre and the Shryves for the towne dyd present her with ypocras, and other wynes, plentye, with soundry kyndes of fysshes. All the which presentes she dyd thankefully resceyve, saing, that she was never able to knoweledge the high honnour and recueill she had resceyved of the Kinges Majestie, and his subjectes. And so, within 2 owres after, by thandes of my servaunte, I dyd resceyve your Lordeships letter, dated the 28 day of the last monyth, which seen the contentes, I made her partely a counseill, touching her sejournyng here, in cace the Kynges Majestie should not come by yesterday to Dover; she beyng right glad and content to followe the Kynges pleasure, making a very good semblant in showing herself, the more she aproches the Kynges Majestie, the glader to be. And so, yesterday ensuyng, the Maister of the Roles, in the mornyng, dyd present her a plentuous dissh of fressh sturgion, and so, by ten of the cloc, she, her gentilwomen, and the said

[1] Sir Christopher Hales, of Hales Place, outside Canterbury.
[2] Thomas Goldwell.

Ambassadour, whent to the Church, where I showed her
Saincte Thomas shryne, and all such other thinges worthy
of sight; at the which she was not litle marveilled of the
greate riches therof; saing to be innumerable, and that if
she had not seen it, all the men in the wourlde could never
a made her to belyve it. Thus over looking and vewing more
then an owre, as well the shryne, as Saint Thomas hed,
being at both cousshins to knyle, and the Pryour, openyng
Sainct Thomas hed, saing to her 3 tymes, "This is Saint
Thomas Hed," and offered her to kysse it; but she nother
knyled, nor would kysse it, but still vewing the riches therof.
So she departed, and whent to her lodging to dynner, and,
after the same, to interteyne her with honest passetymes.
And about 4 of the cloc, the Lorde Priour dyd send her a
present of connys, capons, checkyns, with dyvers fruytes,
plentye; insomoch that she said; "What shall we doo with
so many capons? let the Lorde Priour come and helpe us
to eate theym, to morowe, at dynner"; and so thanked
hym hartely for the said present. At night, she dyd suppe
with thAmbassadour. And thus we remayne, in making
of good chere, tarrying for to knowe your Lordeships
further pleasour. With this, Jhesu preserve Your Lordeship in long lyff, with moch honour. From Canturbury, the
furst day of September.

Alwayes redy at Your Lordeships commaundement,

Wyllm̃ Penison.

## NOTE I

### CAPUT AND CORONA

The first mention of a *Corona*, apart from the narratives of the
murder, occurs in the accounts presented by the Treasurers of
the cathedral for "the year when Prior Geoffry was at the
Roman Court, and Ralph was Cellarer." This was the year 1199
—or, to be strictly accurate, because the financial year of the
convent ran from Michaelmas to Michaelmas, it was the year
from Michaelmas 1198 to Michaelmas 1199. The "oblations"

accounted for in that year were received at seven places in the church. They were as follows:

| | | |
|---|---|---|
| De magno altari | ... | lii$^l$ x$^s$. |
| De sancta Maria | ... | ix$^l$. |
| De Cruce ... | ... | xxi$^s$ vi$^d$. |
| De sancta Michaele | ... | xxiiii$^s$. |
| De Tumba sancti Thomae | | cccc$^l$ v$^s$. |
| De Corona ... | ... | xl$^l$. |
| De Martyrio... | ... | xxxiii$^l$ vi$^s$ viii$^d$ iii$^{qd}$. |

What was the *Corona* here mentioned? Was it a part of the church, like the *Martyrium*; or was it—or did it purport to be— a relic of St Thomas?

That the word was sometimes used to denote the eastern or "crowning" chapel of a church has been well established by Willis[1]. That part of Canterbury Cathedral had been completed, internally, in 1194, so that it was in a position to receive oblations in 1199. It has long been known as "Becket's Crown." It is possible that it already contained objects, apart from St Thomas, which were worthy of devout regard. In the fourteenth century, the shrine of St Odo stood on the southern side of it, and the shrine of the great St Wilfrid on the northern side; perhaps they had been placed there when the chapel was first completed[2].

But the fact that in this list of oblations the *Corona* is placed between the *Tumba* and the *Martyrium* seems to indicate that it was specially connected with St Thomas. And as the *corona* of St Thomas's head had attracted attention from the very time of the murder, and we shall see that something professing to be the *corona* of his head was certainly kept in this chapel at a later time, it appears most natural to suppose that from the outset the name of *corona* had a double significance. The relic may have been set in that chapel because the chapel was the *corona* of the church, and the chapel may have taken that title the more readily because it contained the reputed relic. No long time would be required, to attach to some portion of a skull in the treasury of the cathedral the name of the most sacred portion

[1] *Canterbury Cathedral*, p. 56. Cp. Stanley, pp. 229, 282 f.
[2] See Willis, p. 56. They originally stood in the old Trinity Chapel; and when this was pulled down, they were placed for the time under the *feretra* of St Dunstan and St Alphege respectively: Willis, *ut s.*

of St Thomas's head, and it would seem that the process of attachment was complete within thirty years of the saint's death.

The order of the items on the list is worth noticing. The first four indicate the four chief altars of the original church, and probably represent the form which had been followed by treasurers in the days before the martyrdom. The high altar takes the first place, not only by right of its own precedence, but also because it was flanked by the shrines of the two patron saints of Canterbury—patrons until St Thomas eclipsed them—St Alphege on the north, and St Dunstan on the south. The St Mary is doubtless the St Mary of the north aisle of the nave. The Rood was the great altar of the east end of the nave. St Michael was in the chapel that still bears his name—the Warriors' Chapel. After these ancient attractions of the church come the new ones. The body of St Thomas was still in its *tumba* in the crypt, and if, with Mr Scott Robertson[1], we reckon £1 of that period as equivalent to £20 of our present money, it drew the fine sum of what was worth £8,005 that year. The Martyrdom had obvious claims; but the *Corona* surpassed the *Martyrium* by a considerable sum.

The same order is observed in accounting for the oblations of the next year, and following years. In 1201 to 1204 the Martyrdom stands next to the Tomb, and the Crown comes last. It is probably an accidental variation. The Crown kept well ahead of the Martyrdom in pecuniary result[2]. In 1205 the three items stand in the order, Martyrdom, Crown, Tomb,—the figures respectively being £15, £30, £230. For the ensuing year we have no record. In 1207 the order of Tomb, Martyrdom, Crown is resumed, and the sums received are £320, £27. 5s. 6d., £41. 10s.

After this, the convent were banished by King John, and

---

[1] *Crypt of Canterbury Cathedral*, p. 42.
[2] The figures are these:

| 1201 | Martyrdom | ... £44. |
| | Crown | ... £62. |
| 1202 | Martyrdom | ... £35. |
| | Crown | ... £50. |
| 1203 | Martyrdom | ... £20. |
| | Crown | ... £38. 11s. |
| 1204 | Martyrdom | ... £14. |
| | Crown | ... £27. |

no accounts are preserved until we come to the year of the return, 1213. In that year the treasurers received "by the hand of the Prior of Dover," who was left in charge of the interests of the desolated convent of Christ Church, the sum of £60. 17s. from the Tomb, and £5. 2s. from the Martyrdom. From the Corona nothing was received. For the next seven years the same thing happened. The Corona does not reappear until after the great year of the Translation. The Tomb and the Martyrdom go on bearing profit, as well as the four altars, but the Crown was doing nothing. If *corona* at this time meant the chapel, the fact is inexplicable; if it meant the relic, we may suppose that it had been removed.

In 1220 the *Feretrum*, i.e. the new Shrine, comes into the account, and the receipts stand thus:

| | | | | |
|---|---|---|---|---|
| High Altar | ... | ... | £ 54. 15. 8. |
| St Mary | ... | ... | 13. 4. 9. |
| Holy Rood | ... | ... | 49. 8. 0. |
| St Michael | ... | ... | 14. 0. 5. |
| Shrine | ... | ... | 702. 11. 4. |
| Tomb | ... | ... | 275. 9. 0. |
| Martyrdom | ... | ... | 93. 0. 2. |

The Crown is not mentioned in the account as receiving anything, but as "a twentieth from the Crown" was paid to the legate, Pandulf, amounting to £4. 17s., the Crown cannot have done so badly.

In 1221, after the four altars, four spots connected with St Thomas occur. They are—the *Tumba* taking its ancient place of honour in the order—

| | | | | |
|---|---|---|---|---|
| Tomb | ... | ... | £ 31. 3. 3. |
| Shrine | ... | ... | 429. 8. 0. |
| Martyrdom | ... | ... | 33. 13. 7. |
| Crown | ... | ... | 71. 10. 0. |

Then follows a note in the accounts to say that what was received from the Crown was spent on the Shrine, and a similar note occurs the following year, when the Crown made £80. 10s.

After this follow five years—1223 to 1227 inclusive—when again the Crown yields nothing. It returns in 1228 as the last but not the least item on the list, and remains in the same position in 1229.

With the year 1230 begins a readjustment. The high altar

still holds precedence, with the altars of St Mary and St Michael, but the Holy Rood drops out. The Feretrum takes the first place among the St Thomas localities. At the end of the list St Blaise suddenly makes an appearance, with a contribution of 18s. 8¾d He is, however, but a passing apparition; he is not mentioned in 1231 or 1232, and then after figuring for three years more, he vanishes in 1236 not to be heard of again[1]. Other items begin to waver. In 1231, as in the year before, the Holy Rood is missing, then for twelve successive years it is again mentioned, then begins to come and go; sometimes, even if mentioned, it is mentioned as paying "nothing." Its last appearance, if I am not mistaken, is in 1276. The Lady Chapel begins to show signs of weakness. It passes unmentioned in 1235, 1242; in 1243 it contributes "nichil"; it is unmentioned in 1244. It struggles on again for nine years. In 1254 it is unmentioned; in the next five years "nichil" is its record. Then nothing is said of it till 1275, when it emerges again with "nichil" to its credit. In 1276 it has nothing better to show; it is now the altar "Sanctae Mariae in ecclesia"; this is its last appearance in these lists. A rival Lady Chapel demanded attention. In 1262, along with the four ancient altars and the four St Thomas places, "sancta

---

[1] Our connexion with the Armenian martyr is as follows: Gervase (*Acta Pont. Cant.* p. 350) says that Archbishop Plegmund (890–914) went to Rome, "and bought the blessed martyr Blaise with much money in gold and silver, and on his return brought him with him to Canterbury, and placed him in Christ Church." In Lanfranc's church he had his altar on the upper floor of the north transept, above the chapel of St Benedict, and there presumably his body lay. That floor (see above, p. 62) was removed soon after the death of St Thomas, and it may be conjectured that the offerings mentioned in the text were connected with the translation of St Blaise from an inconvenient situation to a better. In Henry of Eastry's time he lay behind the high altar (*Inventories of Ch. Ch. Cant.* p. 80). Probably the feretrum was placed, like others in the church, on a beam (see *Inventories*, p. 35, and add *J. Stone's Chronicle*, p. 34). The position may be imagined from the descriptions of enthronements of archbishops. Thus Abp. Stafford (1444) after standing at the high altar "passed between it and the altar of St Alphege, knelt beneath the shrine of St Blaise, while the prior said a collect there, and after the collect rose, and knelt before his own seat [the Patriarchal Chair]"; after which he was installed in the seat, and remained there during the offertory, and then returned to the high altar between it and the altar of St Dunstan (Stone, *ut s.*).

Maria in cryptis" enters into the accounts, and there, with few exceptions, she remains year by year till the accounts come to an end. St Michael, who had brought nothing in for some time, ceases to be mentioned after 1262.

To go back to the St Thomas places, the Feretrum is naturally named before the others in the great year of the translation. In the next year the Tumba reasserts for the nonce its ancient precedence, but from 1222 onwards the order (when all four are mentioned) is Feretrum, Tumba, Martyrium, Corona, until we come to 1260. In that year, the high altar stands first, as it had always stood, but it is followed by Feretrum, Corona, Martyrium, Tumba. That continues for many years to be the relative order of the St Thomas places, but in 1264 the high altar itself suffers a drop. The Feretrum takes the first place, the Corona the second; the high altar comes third, followed by the Martyrium and the Tumba. This is the order until the year 1337, after which there is a great gap in the records[1]. When the records begin again in 1371, we find a marked change in the order. The Feretrum still leads, but it is followed by our Lady of the Undercroft, then the Crown, the Martyrdom, the Tomb, and the high altar last of all. In 1374 it is recorded (and not for the last time) that "de magno altari nichil hoc anno," while the Lady of the Undercroft takes precedence of the four St Thomas localities. So things continue as a rule until 1385, when we again lose sight of the annual accounts[2].

So much for the *Corona* in our conventual accounts. But before the time that we have reached—a good while before—a name is mentioned, though not in our conventual accounts, which raises a weighty question. It is that of the "Head" of St Thomas. The "Head" was evidently the principal, or the most popular, relic exhibited to pilgrims, at any rate after the shrine itself. The Black Prince in his will directed that certain of his hangings were to be hung "devant lautier la ou monseignour saint Thomas gist, et à l'autier la ou la teste est, et à

---

[1] 1350 remains: the order is Feretrum, Corona, Martyrium, Tumba; then St Mary in the crypt, then the high altar.

[2] Another claimant of offerings appears for a number of years in the person of Archbishop Robert Winchelsea. In the year of his death, 1313, £50 was received "De Tumba domini R. Archiepiscopi." His popularity, however, was not maintained. The last time that he is mentioned, in 1385, it is to say that he took nothing.

l'autier la ou la poynte de l'espie est[1]": he left nothing separately
or by name to the *corona*. It was the refusal of Madame de
Montreuil to reverence the "Head" which caused surprise to
her conductors. The badges which Canterbury pilgrims carried
away with them as tokens and mementoes of their visit were
chiefly representations, ruder or more elaborate, of a mitred
head[2]. What was this "Head"? Was it something different from
the *corona*; or was it the same thing under a different name?

Let us say, in the first place, that if it were a different object
from the *corona*, and one so important as the actual head of the
saint, it is inexplicable how it is ignored in all our lists of oblations during the years which we have traced. It could not
possibly have been kept separate from both the *corona* and the
body at large, and have failed entirely to attract the offerings
of visitors—or have attracted them without leaving a trace in
the treasurers' accounts.

When for the first time the "Head" is mentioned in our conventual papers, the circumstances point unmistakeably to the
identification of it with the *corona*. The mention occurs in the
treasurers' log-book of receipts—i.e. not in their formal accounts
presented to the convent—for the year 1444-1445. In that
year, John Vyel, who was *custos coronae S. Thomae*, died, on
March 4, while still in office. The treasurers make note of
certain sums received from him, and from his *peculium* after
his death. Then, after some other items, they mention

Et de iiij lib. rec. de Johē Marchall magistro *capitis* sancti
Thomae xvi die Junii.

The next item runs:

Et de vij lib. vj s. viij d. rec. de eodem *Coranario* (sic) in
crastino sancti Thomae.

Then follow three receipts from the Feretrarii, or Keepers of
the Shrine, and then again:

Et de xl s. rec. de Johē Marchall magistro *capitis* sancti
Thomae vj die Augusti per manus Roberti Wendyrton.

---

[1] See Stanley, p. 171.

[2] These badges have been often described and depicted. An
artistic example, preserved in the Guildhall Museum in London, is
given in the Year-book of the Association of Men of Kent and Kentish
Men for 1913–14, p. 49. On the following page is a much rougher
specimen, stamped on the side of a leaden *ampulla* for holding Canterbury water, now in the museum at York. See also the paper by Mr
C. Brent in *Archaeol. Cant.* Vol. XIII. p. 111 (1880).

The natural inference is that *coronarius* is the equivalent of *magister capitis*.

A little further down on the same page is a receipt of money from the Feretrarii " by the hand of Thomas Phylpot," and then:

> Et de xl s. rec. de Johē Marchall custod. Coronae sancti
> Thomae per eundem Thomam (sc. Phylpot).

Either the same man was the keeper of both relics, or *custos coronae* is a synonym for *magister capitis*.

John Marchall died—on the 16th of September of the same year—and the next entry after the one just given is:

> Et de xl s. rec. de Thoma Wakeryng magistro capitis sancti
> Thomae viij die Octobris.

But the word *capitis* has been deleted by the writer, and *corone* written over it[1]. Either Wakeryng succeeded Marchall in one office and not in the other, or the two designations meant the same thing, but the cathedral treasurers considered *corona* to be the more correct or more dignified word to use.

Of these two alternatives the latter is much the more natural. It becomes practically certain when we observe that Stone, in his lists of obits, never mentions a keeper of the Head, though he often records the death of a keeper of the Crown[2].

The same conclusion may be gathered from the somewhat confused account given by the Bohemian travellers in the year after these entries were made, and the conclusion is strengthened by seeing that they locate the Head in that part of the cathedral where the Crown is known to have been. Tetzel indeed records neither crown nor head, but Schassek mentions the head twice over. " We saw there [i.e. in Canterbury Cathedral] his sepulchre and his head." By the "sepulchre" he means the shrine, as the context shows. Schassek proceeds to describe the shrine. Then he says, "There we were shown all the relics." His "there" might, no doubt, again mean "at Canterbury," or "in the cathedral"; but it seems in this place more naturally to mean in the vicinity of the shrine. The "first" item among "all the relics" that he remembers seeing after the "sepulchre"

---

[1] Wakering had been one of the Feretrarii. It would seem to have been a promotion to become Keeper of the Corona.

[2] He sometimes uses the form *coronator* to denote the same office. Hope and Legg, *Inventories*, p. 338, say under the word *corona*, "the famous relic always known by that name at Canterbury, but popularly as the Caput sancti Thome."

was *caput Divi Thomae Archiepiscopi, rasuraque vel calvities ejusdem*; the next object (deinde) was further off: it was the sacred pillar in front of the Lady Chapel. The simplest interpretation of *caput...rasuraque* is that the *caput* itself was so treated as to draw attention to the *rasura*.

That is, in fact, exactly how Erasmus describes the skull as seen by him (if he was not in error)—though he places it in the crypt. *Exhibetur calvaria martyris perforata; reliqua tecta sunt argento, summa cranii pars nuda patet osculo*. Reliquaries of that form are not uncommon. Canterbury Cathedral possessed one which had been completed in the archiepiscopate of his patron, Warham[1]. It was popularly known as "St Dunstan's Head," because a fragment of his skull was encased in it. Penyston's account of Madame de Montreuil's visit supports the view that the "Head of St Thomas" was a reliquary containing the (so-called) *Corona*. The prior "opened" St Thomas's Head for her. The words might of course mean that he opened a case which contained the head, but a simpler interpretation is that he laid open the head-shaped reliquary itself, to show the Corona which it enclosed. Penyston's letter also reads as if the "Head" were not far from the shrine. He makes no mention of taking the lady to the crypt.

That this was actually the way in which the "Corona" of St Thomas was treated is made the more probable by what is recorded of works done in the time of Prior Henry of Eastry (1285–1331). In the year 1314 were expended

Pro corona Sancti Thomae auro et argento et lapidibus
    pretiosis ornanda          cxv li. xii s.[2]

It can hardly be doubted that this great sum—representing

---

[1] See Hope and Legg, *Inventories*, p. 123: porciunculam quandam calve venerandi capitis sanctissimi patronis (?) nostri Dunstani dominus archiepiscopus dicto priori manu propria contradidit ut eam reverenter in quadam massa argentea ac honorifice reconderet Quam quidem massam argenteam in formam capitis dictus prior decenter ac satis artificiose fabricari fecit, in quo eandem porciunculam capitis honorifice ac reverenter fecit collocari, ipsumque inter reliquias ecclesie ut decuit voluit conservari. Quod quidem ab omnibus caput sancti Dunstani vulgariter nuncupatur. The heads of St Blaise, St Fursey, and St Austroberta were treated in like manner; see *Inventories*, p. 80.

[2] Dart, Appendix, p. iii; *Inventories*, p. 39.

two or three thousand pounds of present value—was employed in forming what is often spoken of as the Caput Aureum, or Golden Head, to contain and adorn the Corona[1].

There are, it must be admitted, two items of evidence that the corona and the caput were different articles, but the evidence does not come to much.

Scott Robertson, in his *Crypt of Canterbury Cathedral*, p. 50 (=*Archaeologia Cantiana*, XIII. p. 518), gives extracts from the expense-rolls of the Edwards, showing at what places those kings and their families were accustomed to present their offerings— generally seven shillings at each place. Seven names occur in the extracts—besides the high altar, which on one occasion received from Edward III a magnificent piece of cloth of gold. These seven names are the Feretrum, the Punctum gladii (or punctum ensis, or gladius), the Tumba, the Altare ante imaginem beatae Mariae in vouta (or the Imago itself, once both the Altar and the Image as well), the Chlamys, the Corona, and the Caput. Out of the twelve occasions mentioned by Scott Robertson offerings were made six times at the Feretrum, twelve times at the Sword's Point, nine times at the Tomb, four times at the Altar of St Mary and eight times at her Image, at the Chlamys twice, at the Corona five times, and at the Caput seven times. The order in which the various objects are mentioned is so fluctuating that Scott Robertson's attempt to derive light from it is vain. This is not the place to discuss what some of the objects were. The point that concerns us now is that the offerings at the Corona were made on the first four occasions and on the ninth, those at the Caput on the last seven occasions, and thus on one occasion, and one only, namely the aforesaid ninth, on January 18, 1337, offerings are said to have been made at both the Corona and the Caput. The documents under consideration are not the notes of the offerer; they are entries made,

---

[1] It is surprising that the great Inventory printed by Dart, Appendix, p. iv foll., and more correctly by Hope and Legg, *Inventories*, p. 51 foll., contains no mention of Head or Crown. The explanation seems to be that in 1315, at the moment when the treasures were transferred from one sacrist to another, the Corona was in the hands of the goldsmith, or somebody else, and was not actually received by the incoming officer. This, however, would not, so far as we know, apply to the Sword's Point, which is likewise absent from the catalogue; see *Inventories*, p. 39.

by a clerk at a distance, of monies paid out, in order to be offered in the name of the king, or queen, or prince, by the hand of a servant. On this occasion no offering at the tomb is mentioned. The easiest way of accounting for the entry in 1337 is to suppose that *ad coronam* (or perhaps *ad caput*) is a slip on the part of the clerk for *ad tumbam*. That would probably be undisputed if it were not for the second item of evidence—the testimony of Erasmus.

What it was that Erasmus saw in the crypt can only be a matter for conjecture. That it was not the object known as "St Thomas's Head" is certain from his own description of what he saw in the easternmost portion of the church. If his words *tota facies optimi viri inaurata* stood alone, Nichols might have been right in supposing that he meant a full length picture or image of the saint. There were images of him elsewhere in the church[1]. Large images of royal devotees, like Henry VII, were erected near his shrine[2]. But Erasmus expressly excludes this interpretation by going on to describe the keeper of it as the *assessor capitis aurei*, and as if to make us certain that the thing which brought Colet into trouble professed to be a part of the martyr himself, and not a representation of him, he proceeds still further to say that the prior came immediately after and showed them the shrine in which *reliquum sancti viri corpus quiescere dicitur*. There can, therefore, be no doubt that the *tota facies* was the "Head." If so, there are two possibilities with regard to the object in the crypt. One is that the *corona* had been removed, for the time being, from its reliquary (the "Head") and conveyed to the crypt, which is hardly likely; the other is that Erasmus's memory was for once at fault— either thinking that he had seen in the crypt what he really saw when the "Head" was "opened" in the church above, or thinking that some skull which was shown him in the crypt was St Thomas's, when it was really the skull of another. Sir W. St John Hope suggests that it was the skull of St Dunstan encased in its new reliquary[3].

---

[1] *Inventories*, p. 134 foll.

[2] See Nichols, p. 108.

[3] *Inventories*, p. 123. That foreigners were easily bewildered by the relics presented for their admiration is shown by the remarks of Eberhard Windecke, the devout companion of the Emperor Sigismund on his visit to Canterbury in 1417, who thought—at any rate

Finally we must anticipate the evidence, to be produced in the following section, to the effect that the whole, or nearly the whole, head of St Thomas was found to be in the shrine when the shrine was demolished. One, and only one, professing portion of his anatomy besides the contents of the shrine is affirmed to have been then destroyed. It was "a great scoull of another head[1]." This doubtless describes the so-called *corona* which had long since developed into a *caput*.

The late Father Morris, in his pamphlet on the Relics of St Thomas, had the temerity to affirm that, "until the despoiling," no portion of the saint's head was in the shrine. If that were so, it is indeed inexplicable that no account of the Translation should have mentioned that the head was then separated from the body and kept apart. It could hardly be considered as one of the *ossicula* of which the *Quadrilogus* tells us that Archbishop Langton kept them out. That it was originally buried with the body in the tomb is certain. Father Morris can never have read the accounts of the Translation, or he could not have written that all the crowds who were present on that occasion had the opportunity of seeing the wounded head[2].

# NOTE II

## THE SHRINE

"Two rude representations of the Shrine," as Stanley says[3], "still exist; one in a [mutilated] MS. drawing in the British Museum, the other in an ancient stained window in Canterbury Cathedral." It is impossible to reconcile the two, nor is it altogether easy to say which of the two, if either, can justly claim

in his reminiscences at a later time—that the "Head" was that of St Denys, and that he had seen the "body" of St Thomas, not only his shrine. If Hagen interprets him correctly, Windecke says, "In Canterbury in England sah ich den Leichnam St Thomä von Canterbury und den allerköstlichsten Sarg, den, glaube ich, je ein Menschenkind gesehen hat; daselbst auch das Haupt des St Dionysius." (*Leben König Sigmunds*, § 209, p. 158.)

[1] See below, p. 159.
[2] *Relics*, p. 9.                    [3] *Memorials*, p. 229.

to be a likeness of the work of "the incomparable artists, Master Walter of Colchester and Master Elias of Dereham[1]." Reproductions and descriptions of them, more or less accurate, are given in Stanley, pp. 230 f. and 299 f., and elsewhere.

(1) The former is in the Cottonian MS. Tib. E. viii. fol. 269. It is headed, as Stanley says,

"The forme and figure of the Shrine of Tho Becket of Canterbury."

The description below the picture, restored by Stanley with the aid of Dugdale's Latin translation[2], and of Nichols[3], is as follows:

"All above the stone worke was first of wood Jewells of gold set with stone [covered with plates of gold] wrought uppon with gold wier then agayn with Jewells of gold as broc[hes images angels rings] 10. or .12 together cramped with gold into the ground of gold the s[poils of which filled two] chests such as .6. or .8 men could but conuay on[4] out of the church at [one side was a stone with] an Angell of gold poynting ther unto offred ther by a King of Franc[e which King Henry put] into a ring and wear it on his thomb."

Against the three foliated finials at the top of the shrine are written the weights of them—from left to right:

Siluergilt .60 ounces     [Siluergilt] 80 ounces
        Siluer gilt: 60 ounces

Before the long description is written

Tem: H. 8.

Then at the foot of the page is another picture, of a chest, on the lid of which are depicted what appears to be a piece of a skull with a big hole in it and a small piece inserted in the middle of the hole, and four bones arranged round it. On the side of the chest is written:

"This chest of Iron cont[ained the] bones of Thomas Becket [skull and] all with the[5] wounde [of his death] and the pece cut [out of his skull laid in the same wound]."

We have to consider what is the date of this drawing and whence the information is derived which underlies and accompanies it. The reference to Tem[pore] H[enrici] 8 would

[1] Matt. Paris.
[2] *Monasticon*, Vol. I. p. 10.
[3] *Pilgrimage*, p. 190.
[4] I.e. one.
[5] Or, his.

be enough to show that the picture was not made while the memory of the shrine was very recent. So would the style of the handwriting. But the handwriting tells more than this. I have been favoured with the following letter from the Keeper of the MSS., D. T. Baird Wood, Esq., to whom I wrote on the subject:

British Museum, W.C.
31 May, 1917.

Please excuse my delay in replying. I wished to confirm my own opinion by another.

Mr Gilson agrees with me that the handwriting and presumably the drawing are by Cotton himself. I have compared the hand with Cotton's letters with great care, and characteristic peculiarities confirm the first general impression.

This is, I hope, a complete and satisfactory answer to your questions.

This indisputable judgment carries us one step further. That there was a connexion between this drawing and Stowe's *Chronicle* has long been observed. Stowe's language will be found below, at p. 146.

Nichols (*Pilgrimage*, p. 189) "suspects" that Stowe derived his description chiefly from this MS. Stanley (p. 232) less cautiously affirms that he "evidently" did so. As Stowe's *Chronicle* was published in 1580, and Cotton was born in 1571, this opinion must be reversed. If either borrowed directly from the other, Cotton was the borrower, and Stowe the lender.

There are details, however, in Cotton's description which are not taken from Stowe, or, so far as I am aware, from any other printed work. Of this nature is the information about the weight of the three finials and about the pointing angel. It is not likely that this was a pure invention of Cotton's. The two drawings may have been an attempt of his to aid himself in forming an idea of what the shrine and the corona were like. They were more or less fancy pictures. But the weights—so curiously uninteresting in themselves—must have come from somewhere, and likewise the pointing angel. It is possible that Cotton and Stowe had access to a common authority which is now lost.

(2) The other representation has at least the advantage of being contemporary. The windows of St Thomas's Chapel,

illustrating the miracles of St Thomas, were no doubt made not long after the time of the translation of the relics to the new shrine. The picture in question represents the saint coming out of a gold-covered shrine to visit a man who lies in sleep beneath him. The man is generally said to be Benedict, afterwards Abbot of Peterborough, whose account of the martyrdom has been given above[1]. It might equally well be taken for William of Canterbury. Both men composed histories of the miracles. Both men affirm that they were impelled to the work by nocturnal visions of the martyr. The scale might be inclined in favour of Benedict by the fact that he expressly says that St Thomas appeared to him in pontifical attire[2], as he does in the picture. But how else would the artist have depicted St Thomas if he had the appearances to William in view? The scale might perhaps incline to William inasmuch as his was the later, the fuller, and the more authoritative work, as is shown by its being presented by the convent to King Henry. If so, the scene is supposed to be laid at the Chapterhouse door, where William lay, or dreamt that he was lying[3]. In either case there is a certain anachronism about the picture because while William and Benedict lived, the saint's body was still in the tomb in the crypt: the shrine was not yet made. The anachronism however is a trifle. We may well feel confident that the object out of which St Thomas emerges in the picture is intended for the shrine. Whether it is an exact picture of it is another matter[4].

The drawing of the medallion given in Stanley is not an exact drawing of the medallion as it now is. Perhaps at the date when it was made the medallion was in a different condition. Austin himself certainly left his mark upon the window. He gave St Thomas a new and bearded head, and a bright pink vestment. These have now been removed, and pieces of ancient glass substituted for them. But the chief discrepancy is in the delineation of the golden shrine, or cover, itself. Any one looking at the drawing in Stanley, and comparing it with the Cottonian drawing, is immediately struck by one feature that

---

[1] p. 22 f.    [2] *Materials*, Vol. II. p. 27 f.
[3] *Materials*, Vol. I. p. 138.
[4] It is curious that Mr Austin, in his note given by Stanley, *l.c.*, after noticing the anachronism above mentioned, should proceed to argue from Benedict's description that the shrine must have been open at the bottom, to facilitate the approach of ailing pilgrims.

they have in common, amidst all their differences. The shrine in both is furnished with three conspicuous ornaments on the ridge, one at each gable, and one in the middle. In the window itself there is no ornament in the middle. The two gables are surmounted by finials, but there is nothing corresponding to Cotton's middle finial of 80 ounces. One might guess that it was introduced into the Stanley drawing with a harmonizing intention. The fact is that when the window was first made, there was no such middle finial. It is expressly recorded as one of the works of Prior Henry of Eastry that in 1314 he made "a new crest for the feretrum of St Thomas," costing £7. 10s. (Willis, *Conventual Buildings*, p. 186). We may perhaps congratulate ourselves that Austin—for I take the drawing in Stanley to be his, as well as the note—though he inserted the central ornament into his picture, did not falsify history by inserting it into the window when he restored it. Another change is of less importance. It seems that when he made the drawing, the words *Prodire Feretro* were legible at the bottom of the medallion. I cannot make them out now.

The description given in Austin's note is for the most part correct, but I cannot tell from what source he learned that the body of the saint was exposed to view through doors at the two ends, and that specially favoured pilgrims were allowed to insert their heads through these doors. Erasmus declares somewhat emphatically that this could not be done; and if anyone was allowed such a privilege, we might expect it to have been accorded to him and his companion. For one thing, as Erasmus says, a ladder would have been required to look inside the golden ark; for another, if the golden ark were opened, there yet remained inside it the wooden chest, strengthened with iron, and nailed with iron nails[1], between the eye of the pilgrim and the bones of St Thomas.

It is just possible that the golden object visible in the window is not, strictly speaking, the shrine itself, but the outer wooden cover, which, as we learn from Erasmus, was drawn up and let down by a pulley, disclosing and concealing the golden shrine. The outer, wooden, cover was no doubt handsomely adorned— perhaps plated or gilded. Of this we are not informed. There

---

[1] See p. 71.

is some disagreement between the authorities with regard to the material of the actual reliquary or shrine. The *Polistorie* speaks of the ironbound coffin being placed "under another wooden chest very richly adorned," which evidently means the shrine itself; though the language suggests a moveable cover. The Icelandic Saga, which however considers the shrine to have been constructed after the translation, out of the offerings then made, says that the English people would not hear of anything less precious than gold being used for the material. Matthew Paris in like manner says that it was of the purest gold of Ophir. These expressions however may be satisfied by supposing that a foundation of wood was thickly covered over with precious metal, and do not require us to think that there was no wood at all in the shrine proper. On the whole it seems most likely that the picture represents the reliquary with the wooden cover removed. The repair of the pulley is a recurrent item in the conventual accounts.

The representation in this window recurs twice over at the bottom of the window nearest to the flight of stairs on the south side of St Thomas's chapel. The incident there depicted has not yet been identified, so that it cannot be said with certainty to have taken place at the shrine of St Thomas. The fact that the lady is offering a coil of wire is in favour of supposing the shrine to be that of St Thomas, this being a frequent offering to him—though here the wire appears to be of silver, instead of the usual gold. But even if it took place elsewhere, the shrine and altar of St Thomas clearly influenced the designer. These two little scenes show only half of the golden ark, but the half shown exactly resembles the one above described. The only difference is that the shrine stands somewhat lower than we should gather from the other picture, or from the words of Erasmus. The end of it appears almost to rest upon the altar at which the lady kneels. On the assumption that the shrine is that of St Thomas, the altar, prettily draped with a fair linen cloth, is of course "lautier la ou monseignour saint Thomas gist," as mentioned in the Black Prince's will[1].

No great reliance can be placed on the colouring of the windows, but the arches which support the slab on which the shrine

---

[1] *Inventories*, p. 98. See in Willis, p. 100, the regulations of Abp. Winchelsea for fastening the gates that led to the altar.

rests in all three pictures are coloured red, while the slab, where it is shown, is green. It is possible that the arches—two on each side, as Austin notes—were executed in one of the red marbles which were the gift of Alexander III to the saint's resting-place. A fragment of one of these marbles is preserved in the Cathedral library which must have belonged in some way to the shrine. It appears to have formed part of the square capital or base of a small column. On one side it is flat, but not polished—either to support or to rest upon some other flat surface. The polished portion suggests an interlacing of arches. The stone has been pierced to receive, apparently, metal rods, a larger and a smaller, meeting at a curious angle. It was found, amongst other débris, about the year 1885, in the soil which formed the floor of part of the crypt then assigned to the French Protestant congregation—either the Black Prince's Chantries or the chapel of St Gabriel. Those who gaze upon it may reasonably think that they see the only remaining fragment of the once magnificent structure. The rest of the débris found with it are thought by some to have come from the shrine of St Dunstan, but this is only a guess.

# NOTE III

## SOME OTHER RELICS OF ST THOMAS AND SPOTS AT CANTERBURY CONNECTED WITH HIM

(1) The *Chlamys*.

It is doubtful what this object was, which attracted the devotions of King Edward I. Scott Robertson, p. 51, supposes that it was the same as the *pallium* mentioned by Erasmus (see above, p. 90). This is very probable. Erasmus expressly says that the *pallium* was made of coarsely woven silk. This shows that he does not mean the article of archiepiscopal attire technically called a *pallium*, for *pallia* in that sense are always made of wool. Scott Robertson thinks it probable that in King Edward I's time the Chlamys was exhibited in the crypt. His reason for the opinion is, apparently, that the Chlamys on the two occasions when it occurs is mentioned next to the *punctum ensis*. The argument is not strong. At any rate it disappears from notice until the time of Erasmus, when, if it and the *pallium* were the same, it was kept in the *sacrarium*—i.e. either the Treasury, or the chapel of St Andrew, which is called *Vestiarium* in the plan of Prior Wibert (c. 1160)—and shown only to specially favoured pilgrims. I think that it was most likely kept in the same place and exhibited under the same restrictions from the beginning. It is curious that the Chlamys does not appear in the great inventory of 1315. A *pallium* of St Thomas is indeed mentioned there, but it must have been the *pallium* in the technical sense, for it was small enough to be kept *in parva Cuppa argentea et deaurata* (*Inventories*, p. 84). Possibly the Chlamys is to be identified with one or other of the pieces of garments mentioned on pp. 85, 86 of the *Inventories*, but the way in which it is spoken of seems to require something more complete.

(2) The *pedum* seen by Erasmus would appear to be the same as the *Baculus Sancti Thome de Piro cum capite de nigro cornu* (of pearwood, with a head of black horn) on p. 70 of the *Inventory* of 1315[1]. Erasmus noted its shortness. His description does not seem to agree with that of "one staff of Thomas Becketes sett w^t perle and stone" mentioned in 1540 (*Inventories*, p. 197). A State Paper of that year (1540, No. 809) speaks of "Thomas Bekkett's staff": it may or may not have been the one seen by Erasmus, or the one in the Inventory just mentioned.

(3) The *cilicium*, or hair shirt (subuculum, ein grob hären hemd, indusia cilicina), and to a lesser extent the waistbands (cingula) and drawers (subligaria) of the same material, can be fairly traced throughout the history. Gervase (see *Inventories*, p. 85 note) speaks of St Thomas as being buried in them (he does not specify the waistbands). Sir W. St John Hope is doubtless right in conjecturing (*Inventories*, *l.c.*) that all these articles were removed from the body at the time of the translation—the only occasion, so far as we are aware, that the coffin was opened between the burial and the destruction of the shrine. In 1315 the *cilicium* and part of a *cingulum* were kept in a "big round ivory case, in an oblong *caput* [whatever that was] with a copper lock" (*Inventories*, p. 85): in the same case, wrapped

---

[1] There is another *Baculus Sancti Thome*, silver-gilt and adorned with gems, among the Chanters' staves on p. 74, but this would not be a *pedum*.

in a cloth of white diaper was part of the fastening of the *cilicium* (de ligatura cilicii ejusdem). This fastening and the part of the *cingulum* above mentioned may have been the waist-bands (cingula) in Erasmus's catalogue. We are not told in what part of the church the ivory case was kept. When Rotzmital visited Canterbury, the *cilicium* had been taken out of the case and was displayed. If Tetzel is to be believed it was suspended over the shrine (ob dem sarch hecht); but Tetzel was a little puzzled over his localities. He says that the place where St Thomas was "beheaded" was under the shrine, and the shirt over the shrine. His memory probably confused the Martyrdom with the *tumba*, and the *tumba* with the shrine, and thought that the shirt was over the shrine, when it was really over the *tumba*. There it certainly was when Erasmus came, and the other articles of the same material with it. There it no doubt remained till 1538. It was probably the very *cilicium* which was once mended by the B. V. Mary herself[1].

(4) Schassek records that he saw "a pillar in front of the chapel of the Mother of God, by which he [St Thomas] used to pray and to enjoy conversation with the Blessed Virgin." The mention of it is introduced by the words, "There we were shown all the relics." As these words are preceded by the account of the shrine, it would be natural to conclude from the word "There" that pillar and chapel alike were in that neighbourhood. There is, however, no evidence of any chapel of our Lady in that part of the church, and perhaps Schassek's memory in this particular was at fault.

His companion Tetzel bears out the statement that the object described by Schassek was somewhere in the region of the shrine, though he does not remember the chapel. His recollections of the relation between the various spots is confused, as we have seen; but he passes from the Martyrdom "to a stone chair"—no doubt the Patriarchal Chair, which stood until the 19th century at the head of the steps behind the high altar—"where," he says, "is the figure of our Lady, which often talked with St Thomas." The figure was no doubt erected on a pillar —the pillar mentioned by Schassek. Tetzel then proceeds, "The said figure now stands (stet iezunt) in the choir." This appears to imply that formerly it had stood elsewhere. "The

[1] *Materials*, Vol. II. p. 292.

choir" gives choice of a large variety of sites, but the statement distinctly places the figure, with its pillar, on or about the platform where the Patriarchal Chair stood.

Are we to connect the language of the Bohemian visitors with that of Erasmus regarding the site of the Martyrdom? "There the saintly man is said to have paid his last salutation to the Virgin, when death was close at hand." It is likely enough that that "last salutation" became in legend frequent conversation between the two saints—indeed the word "last" may be intended to imply the thought. Is it not possible that the figure of the Blessed Virgin, of which William of Canterbury speaks (see p. 7), which stood before St Thomas in his last moments, was preserved when the nave and its Lady Chapel were pulled down, and, when the Bohemians came to Canterbury, had found a habitation "in the choir"? At the time of their visit (1446) all the neighbourhood of the north transept was in the builders' hands. The first stone of the new Martyrdom was laid Sept. 9, 1448[1]. The altar of the new Lady Chapel was consecrated on St Luke's Day, 1455.

There is ground for thinking that the figure was moved again. We read in Stone (p. 102) that at the Epiphany season 1467 there was a great outburst of water in the crypt, so that for four weeks the convent were unable to go there in procession, but went instead "to the image of the Blessed Virgin Mary towards the dormitory, which image is between the altars of St Martin and St Stephen." These were the altars on the east side of the north choir transept. The image must have stood on a pedestal or pillar between the two apses. This may have been the very image that conversed with St Thomas; but from the way in which Stone speaks of it, we might conjecture that the image *versus dormitorium* was a less important image than that of the Lady Chapel in the undercroft, and that our Lady of the Undercroft, on whose riches Erasmus dwells with such relish, was herself the one who had received the dying salutation of St Thomas. To her, it seems, there were solemn processions of the whole convent at frequent—perhaps weekly—intervals; and when she was inaccessible, the image in the upper church acted as her substitute. The special veneration in which she was held is shown, not only by the account of Erasmus, but also

[1] Stone, p. 44.

by such legacies as those recorded in *Inventories*, pp. 109, n. 3, 111. Sir W. St J. Hope, at the latter place, seems to prove that the figure between the altars of St Martin and St Stephen was the interesting *mensura beate Marie*, or image which gave the stature of the Blessed Virgin[1].

(5) Both Bohemians mention the spring, or well, of St Thomas. It was, no doubt, the well, or spring, from which water was carried away by pilgrims in leaden bottles. Stanley has given a picturesque and interesting account of it[2]. He refers to the *Polistoric*, of the reign of Edward II, as the earliest authority for it. It may be so. We do not know how early the offices for the festivals of St Thomas were drawn up. But if Archbishop Parker is right, they were the work—or some of them were the work—of St Thomas Aquinas[3]. St Thomas Aquinas died in 1274. The miracle of the well—at least of the water—is commemorated in the Sarum offices for the feast of the Martyrdom[4]. One of the anthems at Lauds is

Aqua Thomae quinquies varians colorem
in lac semel transiit, quater in cruorem.

The miracle of the water was known at a still earlier date. The conversion into milk occurs in William of Canterbury[5]; the conversion into blood, more than once, occurs in Benedict[6]. But the changes did not, in the original accounts, take place in the well, but in the water when carried away by devotees of St Thomas. Gradually the belief appears to have arisen that the well itself was miraculous. Such was the impression made upon the Bohemian pilgrims of the fifteenth century. They seem to have attributed it to the fact that St Thomas in his lifetime drank daily of the well. By the sixteenth century it had become the general belief that the well was subject to these miraculous conversions[7]. No longer was it a drop of the blood of St Thomas

---

[1] *Pictura*, and *picture* in Middle Age English, often denote a coloured image.

[2] P. 235, and Note C in the Appendix. Erasmus has nothing to say about it: he entered the church from the south side, while the Bohemians appear to have entered through the convent.

[3] See below, p. 141.

[4] Procter and Wordsworth, Fasc. I. col. cclviii

[5] *Materials*, Vol. I. p. 354.

[6] *Materials*, Vol. II. p. 189 f.     [7] See below, p. 161.

which wrought wonders upon water with which it was diluted, but the spring itself had received supernatural virtue.

Stanley says that "the well" was probably that which in the old plans of the monastery is marked *Puteus*. He is probably right. The plan of Prior Wibert, to which he no doubt refers, marks the *Puteus* as standing a little to the north of the way leading from the Great Cloister to the Infirmary, not far from the octagonal water tower called in later times the Baptistery. This would answer to the indications of the Bohemian pilgrims. The spring was "in the convent" (Schassek). This, of itself, would exclude any claims of the little well in the crypt, discovered by the late Mr Pugh. It was "on the left-hand side as you go" into the place under the shrine where St Thomas was beheaded, and where his shirt was hung (Tetzel). This, as we have seen, is intended for a description of the crypt and the *tumba*. The Bohemians passed through the convent, it seems, and entered the crypt by the door in the north choir transept. This *puteus* would be, as Tetzel says, on the left-hand side.

Another authority has been made known since Stanley wrote, which seems to corroborate Stanley's opinion. Stone twice over mentions the *fons Sancti Thomae*—though in the former of the two places he or his copyist twice, by a slip of the pen, writes *pons* instead of *fons*[1]. On p. 73 he describes a procession "from the choir, through the nave of the church, through the cloister, by St Thomas's well (*per pontem S. Thome*), and so into the Infirmary Chapel." There mass was said, and a sermon was preached at the door of the *deportum*—we must consider presently what this was—and after the sermon "the convent returned by St Thomas's well (*pontem*), and by the chapterhouse door, and by the shrine of St Thomas, and so into the nave of the church." On p. 85 Stone records a procession to St Gregory's. On the return journey, the procession went "by the Court gate"—that is, by the great entrance from the Mint-yard to the Green Court—"and by St Thomas's well (*fontem*), and by the chapterhouse door, and so into the choir."

All would be clear, but for the mention of the *deportum*. Willis, *Conventual Buildings*, p. 59, explains what a *deportum* was —a kind of parlour—and says, "It is likely that it was placed

---

[1] The present Master of Corpus Christi has kindly verified for me Searle's reading of the MS.

over the Buttery buildings to the west of the vestibule of the Refectory, so as to be in convenient juxtaposition with the passage from the Convent Kitchen." Willis did not know Stone's Chronicle, or perhaps he would have altered this opinion. The door of a chamber on an upper storey would be an unnatural place for a sermon; and if the *deportum* were where Willis places it, along the western end of the north alley of the cloister, between the Refectory and the Cellarer's lodging, the well would have to be placed inside the cloister; because, to get from a *deportum* placed where Willis places it, to the Chapterhouse door, the obvious way would be to enter the cloister straight by the existing Refectory door. Such a position for the well, inside the cloister, is plainly impossible. Unless therefore we are to suppose that for some not very intelligible reason the convent, on the first occasion recorded by Stone, passed from the Infirmary to the opposite end of the Great Cloister to hear a sermon, and then returned (for a second time) half way to the Infirmary before entering the cloister by way of St Thomas's well, we must place elsewhere the *deportum* in question. Either there was a *deportum* belonging to the Infirmary, apart from the main *deportum* of the convent, or else the main *deportum* must have lain somewhere not very far from the natural route between the Infirmary Chapel and the Chapterhouse door.

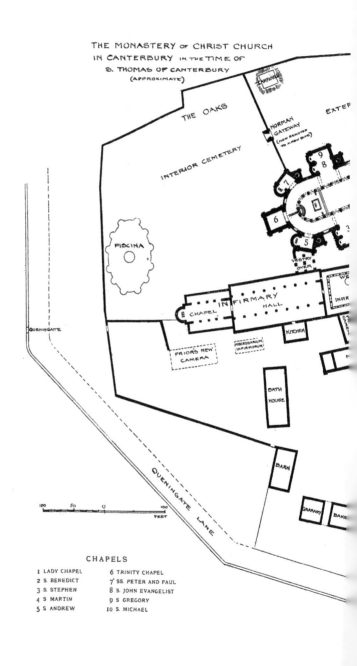

THE MONASTERY OF CHRIST CHURCH
IN CANTERBURY IN THE TIME OF
S. THOMAS OF CANTERBURY
(APPROXIMATE)

THE OAKS

INTERIOR CEMETERY

NORMAN
GATEWAY
(NOW REMOVED
TO A NEW SITE)

EXTER

PISCINA

VESTRY
&
OVER

WE

INFIRMARY
HALL

CHAPEL

INFIR

PRIORS NEW
CAMERA

NECROSARIUM
INFIRMORUM

KITCHEN

BATH
HOUSE

QUENINGATE

BARN

QUENINGATE LANE

GRANARY    BAKE

100    50    0    100
FEET

CHAPELS

1 LADY CHAPEL        6 TRINITY CHAPEL
2 S. BENEDICT        7 SS. PETER AND PAUL
3 S. STEPHEN         8 S. JOHN EVANGELIST
4 S MARTIN           9 S GREGORY
5 S ANDREW          10 S. MICHAEL

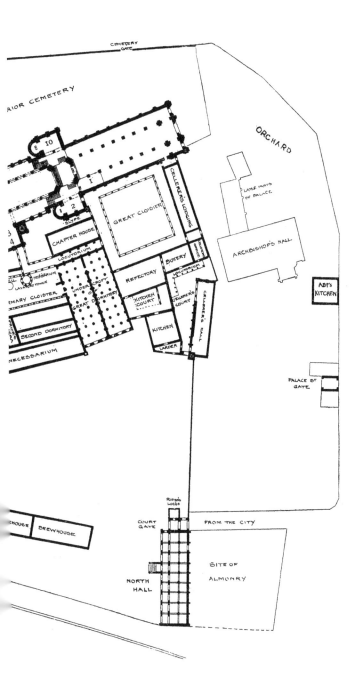

CEMETERY GATE

RIOR CEMETERY

ORCHARD

10

LATER PARTS OF PALACE

CELLERER'S LODGING

ARCHBISHOP'S HALL

ABT'S KITCHEN

CHAPTER HOUSE

SLYPE

GREAT CLOISTER

LOCUTORIUM

HERBARIUM

REFECTORY

BUTERY

LAVATORY TOWER

UNDER CROFT OF GREAT DORMITORY

KITCHEN COURT

LOCUTORIUM

CELLERER'S COURT

CELLERER'S HALL

FIRMARY CLOISTER

SECOND DORMITORY

NECESSARIUM

KITCHEN

LARDER

PALACE ST GATE

PORTER'S LODGE

BREWHOUSE

COURT GATE

FROM THE CITY

NORTH HALL

SITE OF ALMONRY

# SECTION III

## THE DESTRUCTION OF THE SHRINE

# SECTION III

## THE DESTRUCTION OF THE SHRINE

THE destruction of the shrine of St Thomas took place in September, 1538. The process, as will be seen, lasted over several days. Both King Henry VIII and Cromwell were personally present in the neighbourhood of Canterbury at the time. Their movements are easily made out by the documents in the *State Papers*. The fact that they were near the spot gives additional ground for believing that there was no evasion of their injunctions in the matter. Whatever Cromwell on his master's behalf decreed was doubtless executed. Is it known for certain what he decreed?

There was no general Act of Parliament dealing with shrines and relics, nor was there at the moment any general Injunction of the king on the subject, as there was a little later[1].

In September and October, 1541, an injunction was issued to the archbishops which refers in the following terms to the action taken in 1538:

THE KING'S LETTER FOR TAKING AWAY SHRINES AND IMAGES.

(Wilkins, *Concilia*, III. 857, ex reg. Cranmer, fol. 18 a.)

Most reverend father in God, right trustye and right entirely welbeloved, we grete you well. Lettyng you wit, that wheras heretofore upon the zeale and remembrance, which we had to our bounden duty toward almighty God,

---

[1] A passage in Froude's *History*, Vol. III. p. 298, speaks of a "circular" on the subject contained in an unsorted bundle; but the bundles are now all sorted, the Record Office contains no such paper as Froude refers to, and this must be numbered among the deceptive references which are too frequent in that gifted writer.

perceivyng sondry superstitions and abuses to be used and embraced by our people, wherby they grevouslye offended him, and his worde, *we did not only cause the images and bones of suche as they resorted and offred unto, with the ornaments of the same, and all suche wrytinges and monumentes of fayned myracles, wherewith they were illuded, to be taken away in all places of our realme,* but also by our injunctions commaunded, that no offring or setting of lyghts or candells shuld be sufferyd in any churche, but onely to the blissed sacramente of the altare; it is lately come to our knowlege, that this our good entent and purpose notwithstandyng, the shrynes, couering of shrynes, and monumentes of those thinges doe yet remayne in sondraye places of our realme, much to the slaunder of our doings, and to the greate displeasure of almighty God, the same being means to allure our subjects to their former hypocrisy and superstition, and also that our injunctions be not kept, as apparteneth. For the due and spedy reformation wherof we have thought mete by these our letters expressely to wyll and commaunde you, that incontinently upon the receipt herof, yow shall not only cause due searche to be made in your cathedrall churches for those thinges, and if any shrine, covering of shrine, table, monument of miracles, or other pilgrimage do there contynew, to cause it to be taken away, so as there remayne no memorye of it; but also that you shall take order wythe all the curates and other, havynge wythin your dioces chardge, to do the semblable, and to see that your injunctions be duely kept, as apperteneth, wythout fayling, as we truste, and as you wyll answere for the contrarye. Yeven under our signet at our towne of Hull the 4th daye of October, in the thirty fourth[1] yere of our reign[2].

[1] Rectius, "third."
[2] Cp. the following:
"Tharchbishop of York was comaunded to cause all the shrynes, w[t] their hovels and all other their appertenances, to be taken downe in all his provence, and the places where they stode to be made even and playne." Nicholas, *Proceedings and Ordinances of the Privy Council*, Vol. VII. p. 247 (Sept. 22, 1541).

The words emphasized in the foregoing document describe what had taken place in 1538 with regard to shrines and relics[1]. The king's letter says nothing of what was done with them, beyond that they were, or were intended to be, "taken away." In particular no kind of destruction of relics is contemplated. The letter further draws a distinction between the procedure in the case of these objects and that pursued in the case of burning of lights. The burning of lights, except those before the sacrament, was forbidden "by our injunctions"; of the shrines, images, bones, monuments, and "writings" (probably meaning inscriptions), the king only says that he "caused" them to be taken away. He does not specify the means adopted for the purpose.

From the instances which we can trace, we may safely say that the method was in each case the issue of a special commission to particular persons, under the privy seal, authorising them to deal with a particular shrine, or with all the shrines of a particular church or churches. The commissions with regard to St Richard of Chichester and St Hugh of Lincoln may be supposed to be examples of the rest. They are as follows:

COMMISSION FOR TAKING DOWN ST RICHARD'S SHRINE AT CHICHESTER.

(Record Office.)

Henry the eighth, by the grace of God king of England and of France, defender of the faith, lord of Ireland, and in earth immediately under Christ supreme head of the church of England, to our trusty and well beloved servant, Sir Will. Goring, Knight, and William Ernely, Esquire, greeting. Forasmuch as we have been lately informed, that in our city of Chichester, and cathedral church of the same, there hath been used long heretofore, and yet at this day is used much superstition, and certain kind of idolatry about the shrine and bones of a certain bishop of the same,

---

[1] Cromwell, it will be remembered, had fallen in the meantime.

which they call St. Richard; and a certain resort thither of sundry our subjects which being men of simplicity, by the instigation of certain of the clergy, who take advantage of the same, do seek at the said shrine and bones of the same, that[1] God only hath authority and power to grant; we willing such superstitious abuses and idolatries to be taken away, and that from henceforth there shall remain no such occasion, whereby our people and subjects of simplicity may be led into errors; as we have caused in other places such occasions to be taken away, we trusting in your fidelities, discretions and wisdoms, have assigned, committed, and appointed you, and every of you; willing and commanding you with all convenient diligence to repair unto the said cathedral church of Chichester, and there to take down that shrine and bones of that bishop called St. Richard, within the same, with all the silver, gold, jewels, and ornaments to the same shrine belonging; and also all other the reliques and reliquaries of the said cathedral church, and that not only ye shall see the same shrine, bones, and reliques, with all the plate, gold, jewels, ornaments, aforesaid, to be safely and surely conveyed and brought unto our Tower of London, there to be bestowed as we shall further determine at your arrival, but also that ye shall see both the place where the same shrine standeth to be rased and defaced even to the very ground; and all such other images in that church, as any notable superstition hath been used, to be taken and conveyed away, so that our said subjects shall by them be in no wise deceived hereafter; but rather restore and give unto almighty God, and to no earthly creatures such high honour, as is due unto him the Creator of all.

Wherefore we will and straitly charge and command the clergy of the same our city and cathedral church, the mayor, bailiffs, aldermen and other our officers, ministers, and subjects whatsoever they be, which ye shall require, to be aiding, helping and assisting unto you in the doing, fulfilling, and accomplishing of all and singular the premisses,

[1] For "that which."

without any let or interruption, as they tender our pleasure
and will answer for the contrary at their extreme peril.
Given under our privy seal at our manor of Hampton
Court the 14th day of December, in the xxx[th] year of our
reign.

Thomas Cromwell[1].


COMMISSION FOR TAKING DOWN THE SHRINE OF
ST HUGH AT LINCOLN.

(Dugdale, *Monasticon*, ed. 1846, Vol. VI. Part III. p. 1286.)

Henry the Eighth, by the grace of God, king of England,
and of France, defender of the faith, lord of Ireland, and in
earth, immediately under Christ, supream head of the
church of England. To our trusty and welbeloved doctor
George Hennage, clerk, archdeacon of Taunton, John
Hennage, and our welbeloved servants, John Halleley and
Robert Draper, greeting. For as much as we understand,
that there is a certain shrine and divers feigned relics and
jewels in the cathedral church of Lincoln, with which all
the simple people be much deceived and brought into great
superstition and idolatry, to the dishonour of God, and
great slander of this realm, and peril of their own souls, we
let you wit, that we being minded to bring our loving
subjects to the right knowledge of the truth, taking away
all occasions of idolatry and superstition; for the especial
trust and confidence we have in your fidelities, wisdoms,
and discretions, have, and by these presents, do authorise,
name, assign, and appoint, you four or three of you, that
immediately upon the sight hereof, repairing to the said
cathedral church, and declaring unto the dean, residentiaries
and other ministers thereof, the cause of your coming, is
to take down as well the said shrine and superstitious
relicks, as superfluous jewels, plate, copes, and other such

---

[1] A defective copy of this document is given in Wilkins, *Concilia*,
III. 840, as from MS. archiep. Sancroft inter collect. Henr. Wharton A.
fol. 73. Wilkins supplies the lacunae from conjecture.

like as you shall think by your wisdoms not meet to continue or remain there. Unto the which, we doubt not, but for the considerations afore rehearsed, the said dean and residentiaries, with other, will be conformable and willing thereunto; and so you to proceed accordingly. And to see the said relicks, jewels, and plate, safely and surely to be conveyed to our Tower of London, into our jewel-house there, charging the master of our jewels with the same. And further, we will that you charge and command in our name, that the said dean there, to take down such monuments as may give any occasion of memory of such superstition and idolatry hereafter; streightly charging and commanding all majors, sheriffs, bailiffs, constables, and all other officers, ministers, and subjects, unto whom in this case it shall appertain, that unto you, and every of you, as they shall be by you required, they be aiding, helping, favouring, and assisting, as they will answer unto us for the contrary in their perils.

Yeoven under our privy seal, at our palace of Westminster, the sixth day of June, in the two and thirtieth year of our reign.

We possess the following graphic account of the way in which a body of such commissioners carried out their duties in the case of the greatest shrine in northern England:

### SAYNTE CUTHBERT'S SHRYNE DEFACEDE.

(*Rites of Durham*, Surtees Society, pp. 85, 86.)

The sacred Shryne of holy Sancte Cuthbert, before mentioned, was defaced in the Visitacion that Doctor Ley, Doctor Henley, and Maister Blythman, held at Durham, for the subvertinge of such monuments, in the tyme of King Henrie 8, in his suppression of the Abbaies, where they found many woorthie and goodly jewells, but especiallie one pretious stone [belonginge to the said shrine], which by the estimate of those iii visitors and ther skilfull lapidaries [which they browght with them] was of value sufficient to redeme a Prince. After the spoile of his ornaments and jewells, cumming neerer to his [sacred] bodie, thingking to have nothing but duste and bones, and finding the chiste that he did lie in, very strongly bound with irone, then the goulde smyth did take a great fore hammer of a smyth, and did breake the said chiste [open], and, when they had openede the chiste, they found him lyinge hole, uncorrupt, with his faice baire, and his beard as yt had bene a forthnett's growthe, and all his vestments upon him, as he was accustomed to say masse withall, and his met wand of gould lieing besid him. Then, when the gouldsmyth did perceive that he had broken one of his leggs, when he did breake upe the chiste, he was verie sorie for it, and did crye, "Alas, I have broken one of his leiggs." Then, Docter Henley, hereing him say so, did caule upon hime, and did bid him cast downe his bones. Then he made him annswer again that he could not gett it in sunder, for the synewes and the skine heild it, that it would not come in sunder. Then Docter Ley did stepp up, to se if it weire so or not, and did turne hime selfe aboute, and did speke Latten to Docter Henley, that he was lieing holl. Yet Docter Henley would geve no creditt to his word, but still did crye "Cast downe his bones." Then Docter Ley maide annswere, "Yf ye will not beleve me, come up your selfe and se hime." Then dyd Docter Henlie step up to hime, and did handle him, and dyd se that he laid hole. Then he did commaund them to taike hime downe, and so it hapned, contrarie ther expectation, that not onely his bodie was hole and incorrupted, but the vestments, wherin his bodie laie, and wherwith he was accustomed to saie mass, was freshe, saife, and not consumed. Wherupon the Visitores commaunded that he should be karied into the Revestre, where he was close and saiflie keapt, in the inner part of the revestrie, tyll such tyme as they did further knowe the King's pleasure, what to doe with hym, and upon notise of the King's pleasure therin, the Prior and the Monnckes buried him, in the ground, under the same place [under a faire merble stone, which remaynes to this day] where his Shrine was exalted[1].

The following account of the finding of the relics of St William of York shows that a similar method had been followed there:

## St William of York.

### (*Eboracum*, by Francis Drake, 1736, p. 420.)

At the Reformation, the shrine was demolished, and no remembrance left of the place, but a tradition that this saint laid under a long marble stone spotted, in the nave of the church[2]. May 27, 1732, at the laying of the new pavement in the cathedral, I got leave to search under this stone; the reverend the dean and some other gentlemen being present. At the raising of it we found that the stone had been inverted, and by the moldings round the edge it appeared to have been an altar-stone. Upon digging about a yard deep, the workmen came to a stone coffin six foot six inches long, the lid arched, on which was a cross the length of the coffin. When the lid was turned aside, there appeared a square leaden box, three quarters of a yard long, about eight inches diameter at the top, and gradually decreasing to the bottom. In this box the bones were deposited, it had been closely soddered up, but was decayed in many places....There was nothing like an inscription either within or without the box, or upon the altar-stone, that I could find, to denote that it was the saint that we looked for.

These examples would lead us to suppose that a similar commission—we know the names of the commissioners— was issued for dealing with the shrine of St Thomas of Canterbury, that it ordered the removal of the valuables

[1] Cp. the following note on St Bede's shrine: "The Shrine of holie Sancte Beede before mentioned, in the Gallelie, was defaced by the said Visitors, and at the same Suppression, his bones being interred under the same place where his Shrine was before erected." (*Ibid*. p. 87.)

[2] The shrine had stood in the nave.

to the Tower of London, that it gave no special instructions with regard to the treatment of the bones contained in the shrine, that it directed the obliteration of all traces of the place of pilgrimage, that it gave power to deal with all other objects in the cathedral which were thought to be superstitious. We might also suppose that as at Durham, and York, and Lincoln, the bones taken out of the shrine would be buried, with more or less decency, somewhere near the site, but with no mark to lead pilgrims to them again[1].

But before it can be assumed that this was so, it is necessary to consider whether there were any peculiar circumstances in the case of St Thomas which called for a different manner of treatment. Undoubtedly there were peculiar circumstances. St Thomas was not like other saints. He stood, as no other saint did, for an ecclesiastical theory against which Henry and Cromwell had declared war. Two of the most distinguished of Englishmen had recently been put to death for refusing to abjure that

[1] Some writers speak as if the normal way of treating bones taken out of the shrines in Henry's time was to burn them. So much is this the case that it has been conjectured, even by a high authority, that this is the origin of the familiar word "bonfire." Skeat, *Etym. Dict.*, s.v. (1882), after showing by phonetic rules that *bon* must stand for *bone*, continues, "After writing the above, I noted the following passage. 'The English nuns at Lisbon do pretend that they have both the arms of Thomas Becket; and yet Pope Paul the Third...pitifully complains of the cruelty of K. Hen. 8 for causing all the bones of Becket to be burnt, and the ashes scattered in the winds;...and how his arms should escape that *bone-fire* is very strange'; The Romish Horseleech, 1674, p. 82. This gives the clue; the reference is to the burning of saints' relics in the time of Henry VIII. The word appears to be no earlier than his reign."

The etymology is now undisputed. But the history is sufficiently disproved by a glance at Murray's Dictionary (1888) where we find "1483 *Cath. Angl.* 20/1 A banefyre, *ignis ossium.* 1493 *Festyvall* (W. de W. 1515) 105 In worshyppe of saynte Johan the people waked at home, and made three maner of fyres. One was clene bones and noo wode, and that is called a bone fyre." Below, we read "1493 *Privy Purse Exp. Hen. VII*, in Brand, *Pop. Ant.* (1870), 1. 174. To the makyng of the bonefuyr on Middesomer Eve, 10s." Cp. also Wright, *English Dialect Dict.* (1898), s.v. Bonefire.

theory. There would be nothing surprising in St Thomas being singled out for special forms of posthumous reprisal.

It is well known that an opinion soon took shape abroad that measures of this kind were in fact adopted against him. The earliest and the highest authority for this opinion is the bull by which Pope Paul III professed to excommunicate the King of England[1]. A bull of excommunication had been prepared in 1535, but not promulgated. When Henry's proceedings of 1538, or a travestie of them, were reported at Rome, Paul took his suspended instrument down, and forged it afresh. He accused the king of two things with regard to St Thomas: one was that he had instituted judicial proceedings against him, the other that he had burned his bones.

## PAUL III's BULL OF EXCOMMUNICATION.

(Wilkins, *Concilia*, III. 840. Ex Vol. I. Bullar, Rom. edit. MDCLXXIII. fol. 708.)

...Therefore, as the repentance and amendment, which for about three years we have been expecting, has not ensued, but on the contrary King Henry, strengthening himself day by day in his savage temerity, has broken forth into new crimes; seeing that, not contented with the cruel slaughter of living priests and prelates, he has not been afraid to exert his savagery also upon the dead, even upon saints whom the universal church has revered for many centuries; for whereas the bones[2] of St Thomas, Archbishop of Canterbury, because of the innumerable miracles wrought at them by Almighty God, were kept with the utmost reverence in the said realm of England in the city of Canterbury in an ark of gold, after the king had caused the said

---

[1] Dixon, *History of the Church of England*, Vol. II. p. 97, gives good reason for thinking that the bull was never published *in extenso* till long after. But there can be no doubt that it was penned in 1538, and the charges formulated in it became the common property of Roman Catholic Christendom.

[2] The rhetoric here rises in the Latin to the neglect of grammar.

St Thomas, for the greater scorn of religion, to be summoned to trial, and condemned for contumacy[1], and declared a traitor, he has commanded these bones to be exhumed[2] and burned, and the ashes scattered to the wind; thus surpassing the ferocity of any heathen people, who, even when they have conquered their enemies in war, are not accustomed to outrage their dead bodies; and besides this, he has taken to his own use all the offerings fastened to the ark, which were many and of great value, given by the bounty of divers kings of England, as well as of other princes; and esteeming that even by this means he had not done sufficient injury to religion, he has spoiled the monastery of St Augustine in that city[3], from whom the English people received the Christian faith, of all its treasures, which were many and great; and like as he has changed himself into a brute beast, so has he chosen to honour brute beasts as his companions, by bringing animals into the monastery[4], the monks having been expelled, which is a kind of wickedness unheard of and to be held in abomination not only by Christ's faithful people, but even by the Turks;...

In one respect Paul's bull stands alone and unsupported[5] among the documents of the time. Cardinal Pole, then in Italy, can hardly be considered as an independent authority. The information which reached him was common to him and the pope. Yet even Pole did not know, or if he knew he appears not to have believed, in a literal sense, the rumour

[1] Evidently used in the strict sense: St Thomas failed to appear when summoned, and was guilty of contempt of court.

[2] *Exhumari* seems a curious word to use in this connexion.

[3] The pope was right in putting these two things together: the surrender of St Augustine's took place in the same month as the destruction of the shrine.

[4] The place was turned into a deer park. At a later time, for which Henry VIII was not directly responsible, the pope's language about *Turcis abominandum* became more appropriate; the park became a pig farm.

[5] See note on p. 164.

of a sham trial, although it would have given him a fine
topic for declamation. On the other points his opinion and
the pope's were the same. His *Apology to the Emperor*
goes over the points. The comparison will show that the
Bull and the Apology are not independent of each other.

EPISTOLARUM REGINALDI POLI COLLECTIO.

(Brixiae 1744, Vol. 1. p. 102.)

Thou hast heard, O Caesar,—for I speak not of a dark
and unknown matter, but of one known to all men and
published abroad, because of its extraordinary and unique
ungodliness. Thou hast heard what proofs of ungodliness
[Henry] has exhibited upon that sacred body of a hallowed
man, upon the tomb and body of St Thomas. Thou hast
heard of this first kind of sacrilege, how he plundered and
despoiled the shrine which was studded with so many offerings of kings, princes, and peoples. Of this I do not speak....
But that afterwards he should pluck from it the bones of a
man who had died so many centuries before him (to say
no more than this for the present), should cast them into
the fire, and when they were reduced to ashes should then
scatter them in despite to the wind, has anyone ever read
of such an example of barbarity?...

What then will this godly king say, this avenger of the
wrongs of his ancestor. Will he rewrite history? So he has
done indeed. He has made an edict, as if he himself were
the king whose endeavours St Thomas withstood, or as if
now again when he is attempting and accomplishing much
more ungodly things, that holy man were to return to life
and resist him. He composes an edict in which he pro-
nounces St Thomas a traitor; and as if new evidence had
appeared after three hundred years, although such could
not be found at the time when the murder took place, nor
during all the centuries since, to tell the story otherwise
than as history has recorded it, he thus affirms, that he has
discovered that St Thomas brought his death upon himself,
because he violently thrust away by speech and with hand a

certain knight of the king's who addressed him somewhat vehemently, which violence drove the knight to draw his sword and strike the bishop a blow on the head, by which he fell straightway. So the new edict sets the matter forth, and ends by absolving those who refused, by their own sentence, to be absolved—I mean that knight and those who aided and abetted the murder—and condemning Thomas Becket (so he describes the archbishop in the edict) as a traitor....That is why they disseminate the edict among the people, in order to impugn the truth of the traditional history[1]....

So much for that matter. There was in the same city a church in which the body of St Augustine, the apostle of England, famed for his many miracles, was preserved in a splendid tomb, and a most splendid monastery adjoined the church. This king not only overthrew the tomb: he did that first, but he proceeded to destroy the church and the monastery as well; and the place formerly consecrated to God and that saint, in which day and night holy men sang praises to God with thanksgivings and prayers for the welfare of the king in particular and of the kingdom at large, was chosen by him to be a habitation for himself and his animals, after the eviction of these men; for he gave orders to have a deerpark made there for him, and to build a palace out of the ruins of the monastery[2].

[1] Pole had no doubt seen or heard of the Proclamation given below, p. 142.

[2] Cp. Vol. II. p. 233. (To the Constable of France.) Son certo quella averà inteso prima si come la Santità del Papa vedendo crescer ogni dì più la enorme vexation della chiesa di Dio in Inghilterra incominciata, prima contra li sacerdoti, poi contro il popolo, e tandem pervenuta alla nobiltà, in tal modo, che tutto quello, che con estrema crudeltà ed avaritia con le arme in mano contro disarmati si puo fare hora si vede esser stato fatto in quel regno; ne di questi termini contenti li inimici de Dio hanno avuto ardir di incrudelire fino nelli santi suoi, i quali la majestà divina per tanti testimonii de miracoli ha significato regnare seco in cielo già trecento anni; li santissimi corpi de quali hora sono stati con ogni opprobrio tratti del sepulcro, brusciati, ed al vento sparse le cenere con nominarli scelerati e traditori in dispregio de Dio e della sua religione.          (March 16, 1539.)

Epistolarum Reginaldi Poli Collectio.

(Brixiae 1744, Vol. i. p. 102.)

Audivisti vero, Caesar, nec enim rem obscuram aut ignotam profero, sed propter insignem et singularem impietatis rationem omnibus notam et divulgatam. Audivisti quae in sacrum illud sacrati hominis corpus, in Divi Thomae sepulchrum, et corpus, impietatis indicia edidit; audivisti primum hoc sacrilegii genus, cum mausolaeum tot donariis regum, principum, et populorum refertum diriperet et spoliaret. Sed de hoc non loquor....Verum ut postea hominis ossa (nihil enim hic amplius dicam) tot ante eum seculis mortui erueret, igni traderet, in cinerem redacta per contumeliam postea in ventum spargeret, an ullum similis crudelitatis exemplum inter homines unquam est lectum?

(p. 105) Quid ergo dicet hic pius rex, vindicator injuriarum proavi sui? Num novam aliquam historiam condet? Sic sane fecit. Edictum enim fecit, tanquam ipse fuisset ille rex, cujus conatibus Divus Thomas restitisset, vel nunc iterum, cum multa magis impia moliatur et perficiat, cui[1] rediens ad vitam sanctus ille vir obsisteret. Sic quidem edictum scribit, in quo Divum Thomam proditorem pronunciat, et quasi jam recentes venissent testes post trecentos annos, qui nec illo tempore, cum caedes facta est, inveniri potuerunt, nec tot saeculis postea, qui rem aliter, quam in historia scriptum est, narrarent; sic dicit, se pro comperto habere, Divum Thomam suae mortis causam fuisse, qui militem quendam regis verbis et in causam regis eum acrius alloquentem manu a se violenter repulerit[2], qua violentia commotus miles gladium strinxerit, et in caput episcopi vulnus inflexerit, quo statim cecidit. Sic quidem novum edictum rem declarat; quare ita concludit: ut qui suo judicio noluerunt esse absoluti militem illum et quotquot conscii et adjutores fuerunt impiae caedis per edictum absolvit[3], et Thomam Bechet (sic enim in edicto archiepiscopum appellat) proditionis condemnat[3]....Ob hanc enim causam edictum in vulgus spargunt, ut historiae veteris veritati derogent,...

(p. 109) Hoc vero tale est. Cum in eadem urbe templum

---

[1] The *cui* seems to be redundant.
[2] The order of the words seems suspicious.
[3] Pole probably meant to write *absolvat, condemnet*.

esset, in quo Divi Augustini, Anglorum apostoli, multis miraculis clari, corpus asservabatur magnifico sepulchro conditum,
et templo monasterium magnificentissimum adjunctum; hic
quidem non sepulchrum solum evertit, sed hoc primum, deinde
templum una cum monasterio prorsus diruit, et locum prius
Deo et illi sancto viro dedicatum, in quo dies et noctes Deo
sacrati homines laudes cum gratiarum actionibus et obsecra-
tionibus pro illius praecipue salute et universi regni Deo cane-
bant, illis ejectis, sibi et feris domicilium, esse voluit; sic enim
jusserat vivarium illic fieri, et sibi ex ruinis monasterii palatium
aedificari.

Such accusations speedily became current on the continent. Sometimes other saints· were brought into the indictment, besides St Thomas and St Austin. Castelnau
writes to Montmorency on December 6 that the pope's
nuncio in Spain presses for vengeance upon Henry for
his treatment of the relics of St Edward the Confessor, and
St Thomas[1]. Hoby, the English ambassador in Spain,
reports the offence given by "the burning the saint's
bones[2]." Pole lost no opportunity of telling the story.
Sometimes, however, he seems not to have pressed the
point of the burning of the bones, but dwelt more upon
the iniquity of their being unshrined. Thus an informer,
giving evidence before the Council of a conversation which
he had with "Polle" at Rome, affirms:

"We dined at Borobryg's cost, and after dinner Polle said
the hospital[3] was founded in the name of T. of C. whom the
king had pulled out of his shrine. I answered it became
never a servant to be better clothed than his master, and
I had seen the sepulchre of our master Christ and also the
sepulchres of all his progeny which was nothing in comparison with that shrine[4]."

Naturally enough, the accusations of Paul III and of
Reginald Pole became a *mot d'ordre* for subsequent controversialists on the Roman side, both English and foreign.

---

[1] *State Papers*, 1538, Vol. II. no. 995; from Ribier, I. 287.
[2] *Ibid.* no. 974.
[3] Of St Thomas at Rome.         [4] *State Papers*, 1540, no. 721.

Such writers as Nicholas Sander or Sanders[1] and Thomas Stapleton[2] add nothing to the weight of evidence for what they repeat. They were not personally acquainted with the facts. A certain degree of interest attaches indeed to the language of Sander, because for some of his statements he appears to have behind him other authority than that of the pope; but an attentive study of the early editions of his book shows that for the citation of St Thomas (he does not mention the burning of the bones) he was dependent upon the pope's bull and nothing else. The Jesuit Persons, who amplified the work of Sander, quotes from a lost work by one Richard Hilliard a passage on the indignities offered to shrines in general. Persons, perhaps on the authority of Hilliard, speaks especially of the indignities offered to three martyrs, St Alban, St Edmund, and St Thomas; but he does not affirm that the relics of any of the three were burnt[3], except so far as that he quotes the bull of Paul III *in extenso*[4].

The case of another of these controversialists has an interest, likewise, but for a different reason. Nicholas Harpsfield, Archdeacon of Canterbury under Queen Mary, was at one time quoted as a witness that the bones of St Thomas were buried, and not burned. Dean Stanley quotes him to that effect, in speaking of the destruction of the shrine. He takes the passage from Wordsworth's *Ecclesiastical Biography*[5]. The words there run:

"Albeit we have of late (God give us his grace to repent, and see our folie and impietie!) unshrined him, and buried his holie relicks; and have made him, after so manie hundred yeares, a traytor to the king [Henry II], who

[1] See note on p. 164.

[2] *Tres Thomae*, p. 58, ed. 1612. The first ed. was published in 1588.

[3] In Sander, *De Schism. Angl.* p. 187 (ed. Romae, 1586). Ad tumulos martyrum progreditur, quos omnes expilabat, reliquiasque indignissimis modis tractabat.

[4] *Ibid.* p. 190 foll.

[5] The passage in the standard (4th) edition of Wordsworth is in Vol. II. p. 181. Stanley's reference "(II. 226)" is to an earlier edition.

honoured him for a blessed saint, as did all the kings his successors."

It is now, however, ascertained that the *Life of Sir Thomas More* printed by Wordsworth as Harpsfield's is not the original work of Harpsfield, but a compilation by "Ro . Ba.," whoever "Ro . Ba." may be, from the Lives by Harpsfield and Roper. "Ro . Ba." had presumably no intention of correcting Harpsfield, when he wrote the word "buried"; but if not, he misread the manuscript before him. What Harpsfield wrote was:

"Albeit we have of late (God illuminate our beetle blind hearts to see and repent our folly and impiety!) unshrined him and burned his holy bones, and not only unshrined and unsainted him, but have made him also (after so many hundred years) a traitor to the king that honoured him," etc., and then Harpsfield adds:

"Even as they have taken up and burned the bones of blessed St Augustine, our Apostle, who brought the faith of Jesus Christ first into this realm[1]."

Stanley, quoting Harpsfield's supposed reading "buried," calls it an "unexceptionable testimony." A writer who shows that Stanley was wrong in supposing him to have written "buried," claims that Harpsfield's testimony to the burning of the bones is thus admitted to be "unexceptionable." But that is far from being the case. If Harpsfield had really written "buried," his evidence would have been of value, because it would have shown that he was departing from his principal authorities in a case where it would have been to his own interest to agree with them, and therefore he might be presumed to have historical reason for doing so. But as he wrote "burned," it becomes plain that he took his "facts" straight from the pope and the cardinal, without any independent investigation. His

---

[1] Harpsfield's *Life of Sir T. More* has never been printed. There are MSS. of it in the British Museum (Harl. 6253) and at Lambeth (no. 829). My quotation is taken from the pamphlet, *The Relics of St Thomas of Canterbury*, by the Rev. J. Morris, S.J. (Canterbury 1888), p. 26.

"testimony" is therefore historically worthless. As a matter of fact he had read carelessly even the authorities which he followed. As they spoke of burning St Thomas and then proceeded to speak of outrages upon St Augustine, Harpsfield supposed that the bones of St Augustine too were burned—a supposition for which there is no ground either in Paul's bull and Pole's *Apology*, or anywhere else.

We turn now to see what substratum of truth underlay these charges.

There is no doubt that Henry VIII caused special enquiries to be made with regard to the character of St Thomas and the circumstances of his death. The result of a scientific investigation was to bring to light facts which had found no place in the traditional account. History, as Pole complained, was rewritten. One who probably took part in the investigation has left a brief statement of the procedure which the angry credulity of the pope distorted into the procedure of a judicial tribunal. This is how Archbishop Parker sums up his account of his most famous predecessor:

M. PARKER *de Antiquitate Britannicae Ecclesiae.*

(s.v. Thomas Becket.)

Thomas was canonized by the papal clergy for his famous martyrdom on behalf of the privileges of his church of Canterbury, and was buried in Christ Church, first in the lowly crypt, and then laid in a lofty and sumptuous shrine[1] up above: in which his head, kept separate from the body, was called the Crown of Thomas the Martyr[2]. Pilgrims flocked to it from all parts, and brought costly offerings. Wonderful miracles were announced, which are recorded by English and Latin writers who celebrate his

[1] Or perhaps he means the "chapel." "In quo" would be a strange way of describing the situation of the head in relation to the shrine.

[2] On this point, see above, p. 96 foll.

praises; and that he might flourish in everlasting glory, never to be forgotten, the acute theologian, Thomas Aquinas, composed elegant prayers for mattins and evensong in a fine and rhythmical style, to please the ears of the hearer and ravish them to admire him; and these were addressed to him day by day. But notwithstanding all this, after the lapse of some centuries, the king called to his aid the prelates and nobles of all his realm, and by diligent and laborious researches discovered beyond question what Thomas was, what wrong things he had done, and what troubles and miseries he had stirred up in the realm. Accordingly he commanded his name to be clean put out and erased in the public prayer books, where it appeared in many places as that of a saint; because he had lifted himself up with intolerable arrogance above the authority of the king and above the common laws, in excess of what the independence and freedom of the Christian religion or the church is entitled by divine right to demand. But the renown of his pretended sanctity had become so famous and so popular, that the church of Canterbury, in which his shrine stood, had lost the name of Christ our Saviour, which it had borne, as I have said, from its first beginning, and had almost taken that of St Thomas instead. This is always the end of hypocrisy and unreality; time brings out the truth, and falsehood is exposed and falls to nothing[1].

Thomas etsi celebri testimonio martyrii a papali clero pro ecclesiae suae Cantuariensis privilegiis candidatus, et in ecclesia Christi humili primum in crypte positus, deinde sublimiori et excelso ac sumptuoso delubro conditus fuerit; in quo caput ejus seorsim a cadavere situm Thomae Martyris Corona appella-

[1] That Matthew Parker would be employed is not only likely in itself: he was 34 years of age in 1538, had been the favourite chaplain of Queen Anne Boleyn, and was of course well known to Cranmer and other leading people: but his account of St Thomas shows independent research of his own. What he says about the church of Canterbury coming to be called St Thomas's is taken from the Lambeth (MS. 135) Anonymus II (*Materials*, Vol. IV. p. 142). That work was known to Foxe (*Acts and Monuments*, Vol. II. p. 247, ed. Townsend, 1837); not improbably Parker introduced Foxe to it.

batur; ad quod peregrinantes undique confluerent, muneraque pretiosa deferrent, stupendaque edita miracula, quae ab Anglicis Latinisque scriptoribus ejus laudes celebrantibus commemorantur; utque perenni gloria nullaque oblivione interitura floreret, horis matutinis atque vespertinis preces ab acutissimo theologo Thoma Aquinate elegantiori stylo tanquam rhythmo compositae atque concinnatae, quibus auditorum aures mulcerent in ejusque stuporem raperentur, quotidie ei fusae fuerint; tandem tamen, saeculis aliquot labentibus, diligenti ac sedula indagatione, adhibitis totius regni praesulibus ac proceribus, rex, et qualis Thomas fuerit, certo comperit, quam nefanda gesserat, quantasque turbas et tragoedias in regno concitaverat. Ideoque nomen ejus in publicarum precum libris, ut sanctum ubivis decantatum, deleri penitus et obradi praecepit. Intolerabili enim arrogantia et supra regiam authoritatem juraque publica, magisque quam christianae aut ecclesiasticae libertatis immunitas divino jure postulat, se extulerat. Tanta autem fama et celebritate adumbratae sanctitatis suae nomen percrebuerat, ut Cantuariae ecclesia, in qua delubrum ejus situm erat, quae, ut diximus, Christi Servatoris ecclesia ex prima institutione dicebatur, id nomen amiserat, et in sancti Thomae ecclesiae nomen fere transierat. Sed hic semper est adulterinarum et fucatarum rerum exitus; ut, veritate tempore probata, hypocrisis patefiat et in nihilum concidat.

The following documents, by which the king sought to justify his proceedings in the eyes of his own subjects and officers, make reference to these investigations:

### PART OF A PROCLAMATION, DATED WESTMINSTER, NOVEMBER 16, 1538.

(Burnet, *Reformation*, ed. Pocock, Vol. VI. p. 221.)

*Item*, Forasmuch as it appeareth now clearly, that Thomas Becket, sometime archbishop of Canterburie, stubbornly to withstand the wholesome laws established against the enormities of the clergy, by the king's highness' most noble progenitor, King Henry the Second, for the common wealth, rest, and tranquillity of this realm; of

his forward mind, fled the realm into Fraunce, and to the
bishop of Rome, maintainer of these enormities, to procure
the abrogation of the said laws, whereby arose much
trouble in this said realm: and that his death, which they
untruly called martyrdom, happened upon a rescue by him
made: and that, as it is written, he gave opprobrious words
to the gentlemen which then counselled him to leave his
stubbornness, and to avoid the commotion of the people,
risen up for that rescue; and he not only called the one of
them bawd, but also took Tracy by the bosom, and violently shook and plucked him in such manner, as he had
almost overthrown him to the pavement of the church;
so that upon this fray, one of their company perceiving the
same, struck him, and so in the throng Becket was slain;
and further, that his canonization was made only by the
bishop of Rome, because he had been a champion to main-
tain his usurped authority, and a bearer of the iniquity of
the clergy; for these, and for other great and urgent causes,
long to recite, the king's majesty, by the advice of his
council, hath thought expedient to declare to his loving
subjects, that, notwithstanding the said canonization,
there appeareth nothing in his life and exterior conversation whereby he should be called a saint, but rather esteemed to have been a rebel and traitor to his prince.
Therefore his grace straitly chargeth and commandeth,
that from henceforth the said Thomas Becket shall not
be esteemed, named, reputed, nor called a saint, but
bishop Becket; and that his images and pictures, through
the whole realm, shall be put down, and avoided out of all
churches, chapels, and other places; and that from henceforth the days used to be festival in his name shall not be
observed; nor the service, office, antiphones, collects, and
prayers in his name read, but razed and put out of all the
books; and that all other festival days already abrogate
shall be in no wise solemnized, but his grace's ordinance and
injunctions thereupon observed; to the intent his grace's
loving subjects shall be no longer blindly led, and abused,
to commit idolatry, as they have done in times past; upon

pain of his majesty's indignation, and imprisonment at his grace's pleasure.

### LETTER TO THE JUSTICES, DECEMBER, 1538.
(Burnet, *ibid.* p. 224.)

They have bruited and blown abroad, most falsely and untruly, that we do intend to make some new exactions, at all christenings, weddings and burials; the which in no wise we ever meant or thought upon; alleging, for to fortify and colour their false and manifest lies, that therein we go about to take away the liberties of our realm; for conservation whereof, they feign, that bishop Beket of Canterbury, which they have tofore called Saint Thomas, died for; where indeed there was never such thing done nor meant in that time nor sithense: for the said Beket never swarved nor contended with our progenitor, king Henry the Second; but only to let, that those of the clergy should not be punished for their offences, nor justified by the courts and laws of this realm; but only at the bishop's pleasure, and after the decrees of Rome. And the causes why he died were upon a wilful rescue and fray, by him made and begun at Canterbury; which was nevertheless afterward alleged to be for such liberties of the church, which he contended for, during his life, with the archbishop of Yorke; yea, and in case he should be absent, or fugitive out of the realm, the king should not be crowned by any other, but constrained to abide his return. These, and such other detestable and unlawful liberties, nothing concerning the common weal, but only the party of the clergy, the said Thomas Beket most arrogantly desired and traitorously sued to have, contrary to the laws of this our realm[1].

It will be observed that none of these documents—neither Archbishop Parker's calm statement, nor the royal denuntiations—give any hint of a destruction of the bones that were taken from the shrine. But there is one line of

---

[1] The same proclamation warns against "sacramentaries and anabaptists." Foxe dates it 1539, and Wilkins copies it from Foxe.

contemporary native evidence for the papal belief that they were burnt. It is the evidence which clusters round Wriothesley's *Chronicle*. Wriothesley's words are these:

WRIOTHESLEY'S *Chronicle*.

(Vol. I. p. 86, ed. Camden Society.)

Allso Saint Austens Abbey, at Canterbury, was suppressed, and the shryne and goodes taken to the Kinges treasurye, and St. Thomas of Canterburies shryne allso, and the monkes commaunded to chaunge theyr habettes, and then after they should knowe the Kinges further pleasure; and the bones of St. Thomas of Canterbury were brent in the same church by my Lord Crumwell. They found his head hole with the bones, which had a wounde in the skull, for the monkes had closed another skull in silver richly, for people to offer to, which they sayd was St. Thomas skull, so that nowe the abuse was openly knowne that they had used many yeres afore; allso his image was taken downe that stoode at the high aulter at St. Thomas of Acres, in London, by my Lord Crumwells commandement, and all the glaswindowes in the sayd church that was of his story was taken downe, with the image of his puttinge to death that was at the aulter, where the sayinge was, that he was borne allso, so that there shall no more mention be made of him never.

In the margin are the notes "In September 1538[1]" and "Thomas Beckets bones burnt and his shryne destroyed." There is no means of knowing whether these marginal notes are Wriothesley's own or the copyist's.

A certain measure of suspicion attaches to the evidence of the *Chronicle*, as we now have it, inasmuch as there are places where, as its editor, W. D. Hamilton, says, it has been "tampered with," to bring it into accordance with Stow's *Annales*[2]. The only existing MS. of Wriothesley,

[1] If Wriothesley himself made this marginal note, it would naturally be at a later time. I have observed no other such note of date in the *Chronicle*.

[2] Wriothesley's *Chronicle*, Vol. I. Introduction, p. xxi.

now in the possession of the Duke of Northumberland, belongs to the end of the 16th or commencement of the 17th century[1]. Mr Hamilton conjectures that it may be the transcript from Wriothesley's original made by E. Howes, who re-edited Stow's *Annales* in 1615 and 1631. The edition of Stow with which the transcriber (whoever he was) was acquainted was the edition of 1592[2].

The relation between the various Chronicles of that period presents an intricate literary problem which has not yet been fully worked out, though the student of the problem will find help in Mr Hamilton's Introduction to Wriothesley, and in the articles in the *Dictionary of National Biography* on Stow, Holinshed and the rest. Mr Hamilton thinks that Stow himself was not acquainted with Wriothesley's *Chronicle*, but that Francis Thynne, who assisted Holinshed, was[3]. If that is so, then Wriothesley and Stow would seem to have had access to some common source of information. The reader will hardly doubt that there is a definite connexion, even if an indirect one, between the passage given above from Wriothesley, and the following from Stow and Holinshed.

### Stow's *Chronicle* (1580).

#### (p. 1013 f.)

Saint Austins Abbey at Canterbury was suppressed, and the Shrine and goodes taken to the Kings treasurie, as also the Shrine of Thomas Becket in the Priory of Christ Church, was likewise taken to the Kings use, and his bones scull and all, which was there found, with a peece broken out by the wound of his death, were all brent in the same Church by the Lord Cromwell. The Monkes there were commanded to change their habites &c.

---

[1] *Ibid.* p. xviii.

[2] *Ibid.* p. xx. Hamilton says that this edition is "only to be found in the Lambeth Library"; but there is now, if there was not in his time, a copy in the British Museum also.

[3] *Ibid.* p. xxi; cp. p. xviii f.

Stow's *Annales*.

(Ed. E. Howes, 1615, p. 575.)

S. Austines abbey at Canterbury was suppressed, and the shrine and goods taken to the kings treasury, as also the shrine of Thomas Becket in the priory of Christ church, was likewise taken to the kings vse. This shrine was builded about a mans height, all of stone, then vpward of timber plain, within y^e which was a Chest of yron, cõtaining the bones of Thomas Becket, scull and all, w^e the wounde of his death and the peece cut out of his scull layde in the same wound. These bones (by commandement of the L. Cromwell) were then and there brent, y^e timber worke of this shrine on the outside was couered with plates of gold, damasked w^e gold wier, which ground of gold was againe couered with iewels of golde, as rings, 10. or 12. cramped with golde wyer, into the sayd grounde of golde many of those rings hauing stones in them, brooches, images, angelles [and other]¹ precious stones, and great pearles, &c. The spoyle of which shrine, in golde and precious stones, filled two great chestes, such as sixe or seauen [6 or 8]¹ strong men coulde doe no more, then conueie one of them at once out of the Church. The monks of that Church were commaunded to change their habites, into the apparell of secular Priests.

Holinshed's *Chronicle*.

(Ed. Hooker, 1586, Vol. III. p. 945².)

Saint Augustins abbeie at Canturburie was suppressed, and the shrine and goods taken to the kings treasurie, as also the shrine of Thomas Becket in the priorie of Christ's church was likewise taken to the kings vse, and his bones, scull and all, which was there found, with a peece broken out by the wound of his death, were all burnt in the same

---

¹ The edition of 1592 has the words here given in brackets.

² This edition of Holinshed—the first which contains this statement —acknowledges in the margin that it was taken by Abraham Fleming from John Stow.

church by the lord Cromwell. The monks there were
commanded to change their habits, &c.

In spite of the hesitations of Wriothesley's editor, let it
be assumed that both Stow and Holinshed were acquainted
with Wriothesley's manuscript, or with the collections on
which it is based. The entry in Wriothesley reads like a
contemporary note. The very fact that the writer does
not specify what church the shrine of St Thomas stood in
is in favour of this view—everybody then knew where it
was. So is the reprobation of the monks for their imposture
in regard to the skull. So is the conclusion, that "there shall
no more mention be made of him never." These are quite
in the manner of the moment. And so far as Wriothesley
goes there are no reserves or modifications in his statement.
He was clearly under the impression that the contents of
the shrine were burnt, and burnt inside "the same church,"
and apparently by the hands of Cromwell himself, not only
as Stow put it in his later work "by commandment of the
Lord Cromwell." If we had only Wriothesley's *Chronicle*
to go by, this part of the papal accusation would seem to
be justified, and the bones—all the bones—of St Thomas
were destroyed by fire.

But there is no reason to suppose that Wriothesley was
better informed on the point than most other intelligent
Englishmen of his time. Although a first cousin of his was
one of the agents in the demolition, the cousins do not
appear to have been on terms of much intimacy. It is
doubtful whether any part of Charles Wriothesley's information was derived directly from Thomas, afterwards
Earl of Southampton. It was more probably the common
talk of London society, which did not discriminate between
the fate of the real relics of St Thomas and the fate of the
spurious ones[1].

[1] In a paper in the *Month* for January 1908 the Rev. J. H. Pollen,
S.J., makes extracts from various State Papers to prove that Wriothesley was himself present in Canterbury and took an active part
in the demolition of the shrine. Mr Pollen is guilty of the almost
incredible mistake of supposing that the Chronicler was none other

We come now to certain documents which have a dramatic interest. Some of them come from the very men engaged in destroying the shrine, who knew exactly what was done. We may lament that on some points they were not more explicit in their statements.

It is clear that Thomas Wriothesley, afterwards Lord Southampton, and Richard Pollard, and perhaps John Williams with them, were the commissioners for the purpose of the demolition[1].

than Thomas Wriothesley, afterwards Earl of Southampton. Thomas Wriothesley, as we shall see, had a share in the transaction, but there is not the smallest reason to suppose that his cousin Charles, the chronicler, was in any way concerned in it.

[1] The second volume of State Papers for 1538 contains the following items that throw light upon the doings at Canterbury and the movements of the persons concerned.

No. 255. Tuke to Cromwell. London, Sept. 1.
(the abbey of St Austin's, Canterbury, is now surrendered, and his Majesty is in those parts [i.e. at Calais].)

No. 257. Peniston to Cromwell. Canterbury, Sept. 1.
(Mᵐᵉ de Montreuil's visit: "content to stay till the king comes to Dover.")

No. 296. Lord Lisle to his wife. Canterbury, Sept. 7.
("that I should not go till the king departed out of Calais.")

No. 303. Husee to Lady Lisle. Dover, Sept. 8.
(Pollard at the shrine; the king at Calais.)

No. 317. The same to the same. Dover, Sept. 10.
(Pollard busy at the shrine; the king at Dover.)

No. 323. Palmer to Cromwell. Calais, Sept. 10.
(the king said to be at Dover.)

No. 350. Husee to Lady Lisle. London, Sept. 15.
(Mr Wriothesley and Mr Williams at the Court.)

No. 353. Pollard to Cromwell. Reading, Sept. 15.
(Pollard at Reading.)

No. 401. Pollard, Wriothesley, and Williams to Cromwell. Winchester, Saturday [Sept. 21].
(Destruction of shrine of St Swithun.)

No. 418. The King to Queen of Hungary, Regent of Flanders.
(No date. Wriothesley to go to Queen of Hungary.)

No. 430. Husee to Lord Lisle. London, Sept. 26.
(Mr Wriothesley and Mr Pollard have been at Winchester "about such the king's affairs as they had at Canterbury," but came home yesterday.)

The first account of what these men did at Canterbury is found in the record of the King's Payments for the month of September, 1538, where, on the same page as a payment in connexion with Madame de Montreuil's visit to Canterbury, occurs a sinister entry relating to the shrine of St Thomas.

## THE KING'S PAYMENTS.

(Arundel MS. 97, p. 34.)

Item payde to Sir William Pennyson knyght by the kingis commaundement certified by my lorde Pryviseales[1] l͠re [i.e. letter] by waye of his gracis rewarde the somme of xl¹¹ for his attendance uppon madame de Montrelly and certeyne other ffrenche ladys com̃ynge owte of Scotlandde boothe at their beynge in London and in their iorney fromme thens to Dover the somme of
} xl¹¹

. . . . .

Item to Mr Writhesley by the kinges com̃aundᵗ certifyed by my lorde privisealis l͠re iiii¹¹ for so muche money by him debursed to these p̱sons folowĩg that is to sey to a sr̃unte of mr Halis m̃r of the Rols[2] for the bringing owte of the Ile of Tenet of one Henry King xxˢ, and to twoo sr̃untes of the busshop of Thetford for brynge one Gervis Tyndale xlˢ and to the saide Geffrey for his cost com̃ynge and retornynge and tarringe at lewis ii or iii days xiiˢ viᵈ
} iiii¹¹ iiˢ viᵈ

No. 434. The same to the same. London, Sept. 27.
(Mr Wriothesley now going to Calais.)
No. 442. Wriothesley to Cromwell. Newington, Sept. 27.
(en route for Flanders: met Bishop Gardiner near Sitting-bourne.)
No. 542. Knight to Cromwell. Valenciennes, Oct. 5.
(talk about St Thomas: Wriothesley's instructions.)

[1] Cromwell.
[2] Sir Christopher Hales had been at Canterbury to receive the surrender of St Augustine's Abbey.

Item payde to the saide Mr Writhesley by like
tr͞e and lyke commaundem͞et xxiii li xvi s for so-
moch money by him layde oute in sonndry per-
cells by way of his maiestes rewarde vnto sonndry
monkes and chief officers of Christchurch in Cant͡-
bery and also to sonndry sr͞utes and labourers
traveling abowte the disgarnisshinge of a shryne
and other thinges there the somme of

xxiii^li xvi^s

It is impossible to read without emotion the next two
documents. They are letters of a certain John Husee, or
Hussey, then at Dover, to Lady Lisle, wife of the Deputy
of Calais. To sit and peruse them is like watching the
burglars at work. Husee's references to what was going
on at Canterbury are jocular. To him the business at the
shrine was only a tiresome hindrance which prevented his
master from gaining the attention of Richard Pollard to
a matter which he considered to be of far greater importance, in which Pollard's influence was desired[1].

HUSEE TO LADY LISLE.

(State Papers, 1538, Vol. II. no. 303.)

Sept. 8 (Dover).

My lord is so entertained[2] with the kings majesty and
my lord privy seal specially and with all others that he is
not like to depart till the kings highness be removing from
Canterbury. His lordship hath promised to be earnest in
his own cause[3], for if the time be now slackyd, it is to be
doubted when such another shall succeed. I have had[4]
his lordship often enough in remembrance....
As touching Mr Pollard, he hath been so busied both
night and day in prayer with offering unto S. T. shryne
and head with other dead reliques that he could have no
idle worldly time to peruse your ladyship's book for the
draught of your ladyship's letters which must be signed

---

[1] I have transcribed them from the originals in the Record Office.
[2] I.e. occupied.
[3] It was some question relating to his illegitimacy. He was a
bastard son of Edward IV.    [4] I.e. put.

for the stay of your great matter. However when his
spiritual devotion is past, I doubt not but he will at one
time or other apply[1] his worldly causes accustomed,
amongst the which I trust your ladyship's shall not be the
last. He hath the book and supplication by my lord's
commandment. I think there be no doubt in the man.
I think this late devotion hath stablished his conscience
that he will use nothing but right with indifferency.

(State Papers, ibid. 317.)

Sept. 10 (Dover).

Mr Pollard hath promised to rid me within ii or iii days
with the king's letters; howbeit I have no trust thereunto
till the king draweth near London....As for my lord he hath
lain every night in my lord privy seal's lodgings, and was
never out of his company but when he went unto the king.
So far there is now no fault for attendance to be found in
my lord....Mr Pollarde hath so much ado with Saint Thomas
shrine in offering and praying that he cannot yet intend to
follow worldly causes, but I trust when he hath prayed and
reshryned[2] the offerings and reliques he will be at leisure.

It is not, of course, to be supposed that there was any
intention of "reshrining" the bones of St Thomas. This
is Mr Husee's humorous way of describing the process by
which the riches of the shrine were to be conveyed to their
new destination; but it seems at least to imply that there
was some special treatment of the "reliques" as well as
for the "offerings." One thing will be noted in these letters.
They give no hint that the Lord Privy Seal was himself
taking an active part in the proceedings at the shrine. If it
had been literally true that "the bones of St Thomas of
Canterbury were brent in the same church by my Lord
Crumwell," it would have been quite in Husee's manner
to have made some amusing reference to the fact.

[1] Attend to.
[2] The State Papers read the word as "received" (resceyved), but
it is really "reshryned."

That the bones were treated more sympathetically by Wriothesley and Pollard than they would have been treated by Cromwell himself is unlikely. Their letter from Winchester a few days later shows the spirit in which they went to work there with the shrine of St Swithun and other things.

### LETTERS RELATING TO THE SUPPRESSION OF MONASTERIES.

(Camden Society, p. 218).

Pleaseth your lordship to be advertised, that this Saturdaye[1], in the mornyng, aboutes thre of the clok, we made an ende of the shryne here at Wynchestre. There was in it no pece of gold, ne oon ring, or true stone, but al greate counterfaictes. Nevertheleswe think the sylver alone thereof woll amounte nere to twoo thousande markes.... We found the prior, and all the convent, very conformable; having assistentes with us, at the openyng of our charge to the same, the mayre, with 8 or 9 of the best of his brethern, the bisshops chauncelour, Mr doctour Craiforde, with a good apparaunce of honest personages besides....We have also this mornyng, going to our beddes warde, vieued thaulter, whiche we purpose to bring with us. It wol be worthe the taking downe, and nothing therof seen; but such a pece of work it is, that we thinke we shal not rid it, doing our best, befor Monday night, or Tuesdaye mornyng, which doon we entende, both at Hide and St Maryes, to swepe awaye all the roten bones that be called reliques; which we may not omytt, lest it shuld be thought we cam more for the treasure thenne for avoiding of thabomynation of ydolatry.

This letter is signed by all three commissioners, but the writer was Thomas Wriothesley, who apologizes for its "rudeness," on the ground that he wrote it in haste, in the church, when he was weary. Within a week of writing it, he encountered Bishop Stephen Gardiner returning

[1] No doubt Sept. 21.

from his embassy abroad. He did not tell him what he had
been doing in his cathedral at Winchester, but he enquired
anxiously of his companion, Thirlby, what Gardiner had
said about the proceedings at Canterbury, through which
Gardiner and Thirlby had just passed. He gives Cromwell
an account of the meeting. The letter was written on
September 27, at Newington in Kent.

(State Papers, 1538, Vol. ii. no. 442.)

This Friday before noon I met with my lord of Winchester between Sittingbourne and Rochester[1]....Then Mr
Thirlby[2] rode a little back with me, and of him I demanded
why he had tarried so long to attend upon my lord of
Winchester. He said their letters were that they should
return together, and as he could not therefore have departed from him but with a great demonstration of un-
kindness, so he would fain have had my lord of Winchester
to have made more haste than he did, and for his own part
hasted so fast that all my lord's train was angry with him.
I asked him what news and how my lord liked our doings
here. He told me that he said he misliked not the doing
at Canterbury, but rather seemed to like it, saying that
if he had been at home he would have given his counsel to
the doing thereof, and wished that the like were done at
Winchester.

Wriothesley, who was on a mission to the Court of Brussels, reached Flanders. From Valenciennes his companion
Thomas Knight wrote to Cromwell on October 5, giving an
account of their progress.

(State Papers, *ibid.* no. 542.)

The people seemeth very superstitious, setting up candles
in lanterns at noondays before images openly in their
"semitories." but this is old. At Bruges a priest told me

---

[1] Here follows a long description of the bishop's great train, and
of the elaborate courtesies between the bishop and him.

[2] Afterwards Bishop of Westminster, Norwich, and Ely.

that there they take the bishop of Rochester and "thother[1]" for holy martyrs and calleth them saints, and said
moreover that the stationer had sundry "epitaphies" of
them both with the description of their lives of divers men's
setting forth. I would have known the authors of those
works, but the stationer was not at home....Every man that
hearkeneth for news out of England asketh what is become
of the saint of Canterbury. But Master Wriothesley who
played a part in that play had before sufficiently "instruct" me to answer such questions. This I write more
to satisfy my bounden duty towards your lordship than
that I think any part hereof worth reading.

It is a pity that the writer did not say more explicitly
what he was "instruct" to answer.

Wriothesley's last reference to the subject is contained
in his despatch from Flanders on Nov. 20.

(State Papers, *ibid.* no. 880.)

That Saturday night supped with us the Marquis of
Barrowe[2], who seemeth well affected towards your Highness, who also declared unto us that it was thought in
these partyes [parts] of many that all Religion was extinct
in England, and when we came to the word of Religion
he expounded it that it was reaported that with us we had
no mass, that saints were burned, and all that was taken
for holy thereby subverted. We declared in such wise the
Religion of your Majesty, the abuses of Canterbury,
Boxley[3], and other places, that he seemed much to rejoice
"thone" and to detest "thother."

But the king's ambassadors were still troubled over the
matter for a good while after. The following shows that in
some cases, at any rate, ambassadors were supplied with
copies of the letter to the king's justices.

---

[1] Fisher and More.                    [2] Bergh.
[3] A famous imposture, of which Charles Wriothesley gives an
account in *Chronicle*, I. 74, 75.

Jan. 7. WYATT TO CROMWELL FROM TOLEDO.

(State Papers, 1539, no. 11.)

I humbly thank you also for your advises off news/by yᵉ lord it is a notable grace that the kyng hath ?crᵈ had the discouery of conspirations agaynst hym. I can not tell (but that god claimith to be pryncypall) wither he hath cawse more to alow his fortune or his ministers. I wold I cowld perswade these preachers aswell to preach his grave procedyng agaynst the sacramentarys and ana-baptistes[1] (as your lordship wrytyth) as they do the burning of the bishopps bones. But of that nor off other news on my fayth I have no letteres from no man but from you.

These last words of Wyatt need not be taken to be an admission on his part that "the bishop's bones" had really been burned. He is referring rather to the foreign stricture than to his own line of defence. From the way in which Thomas Wriothesley couples Canterbury with Boxley, we should expect that the main point on which the apologists were instructed to insist was that the relics which were destroyed were an imposture, pretending to be what they were not. We shall see that this is a right conjecture by the papers that follow.

Two weighty witnesses remain to be heard.

To justify the king's proceedings in the matter of reli-gion, an explicit statement was drawn up at the end of 1538 or the beginning of the following year. It has long been known to historical students by Collier's copy of it in his *Ecclesiastical History of Great Britain*[2]. It is not certain who drew it up, but the existing draft is in the handwriting of Thomas Derby, the clerk of the Privy Council[3]. From the fact that it is headed by a text, it has been surmised to be a set of notes for a sermon to be preached at St Paul's Cross or elsewhere; but this is only a guess.

---

[1] See above, p. 144.    [2] Ed. 1846, Vol. IX. p. 162 foll.
[3] State Papers, 1539, no. 402.

It is more likely to have been intended for distribution on the continent by ambassadors and their agents, like those just mentioned. It must be considered an official reply to the calumnies of the papal party. The account of St Thomas's career and its ending is the same as we have already seen in official utterances of the time. Those who prepared it knew their facts, and it will be seen that they positively and somewhat indignantly deny the burning of St Thomas's bones. The only thing that was burnt was a "feigned fiction," namely, the "head" that was never in the shrine[1].

### PRIORIS PETRI TERTIO.

Dominum Christum sanctificate in cordibus vestris semper parati ad satisfactionem omni poscenti vos rationem de ea quae in vobis est spe et fide.

A sumarie declaration of the faith vses and observations in England.

· · · · ·

Other proceedings of England, the which although they be godly, yet calumniaters do diffame and slander the nation thereby, saying that Englishmen have put down the Christian Religion, churches, holy days, pardons, images, and brent holy Saints and reliques, and martyred holy men, which is a very slanderous and false diffamation, as it shall appear by the truth of their doings as followeth.

· · · · ·

As for shrines, capses, and reliquaries of Saints so called, although the most were nothing less, forasmuch as his highness hath found other idolatry or detestable superstition used thereabouts, and perceived that they were for the most part but feigned things, as the blood of Christ so called in some places was but a piece of red silk enclosed in a thick glass of crystalline, in another place oil coloured of *sanguis draconis*, instead of the milk of our Lady a piece of chalk or of ceruse, our Lady's girdles, the verges of

---

[1] My transcript is taken direct from the original in the Record Office.

Moyses and Aaron, and other innumerable illusions, superstitions, and apparent deceits and moe of the holy cross than three carres may carry, his majesty therefore hath caused the same to be taken away and the abusive parts thereof to be brent, the doubtful to be set and hidden honestly away for feare of idolatry.

As for the shrine of Thomas Becket sometime Archbishop of Canterbury, which they called St Thomas, by approbation it appeareth clearly that his common legend is false, and that at the time of his death and long afore, he was reconciled to king Henry the second, king of this realm, duke of Normandy and Guyenne, and had no quarrel directly with him, but only against the Archbishop of York; which rose for proud preeminence between them, and by the strife thereof procured frowardly his own death, which they untruly called martyrdom. And happened upon a (*sic*) tharrest of a servant of his, whereupon the gentlemen that arrested him caused the whole city rise up [in] arms. And for that he gave opprobrious words to the gentlemen which then counselled him to leave his stubbornness and to avoid out of the way, and he not only called the one of them bawd but also took another by the bosom and violently shook and plucked him in such manner that he had almost overthrown him to the pavement of the church, so that upon this fray the same moved and chafed struck him, and so in the throng Becket was slain. And that he never did act in his life sufficient to prove any holiness, but came to be the king's chancellor by money, was a great warrior, brenner of towns, crocher of benefices, a hunter and a hawker, proud and seditious, by corruption and unlawful means obtained the archbishopric of Canterbury, as he himself confessed openly to pope Alexander, and as by writings and cronikes of good record by his chaplains and brethren the bishops of England made, and sundry of them above a xl years printed in Paris and never reproved (although the mercy of God might be extended unto him), yet nevertheless it was arrested that his shrines and bones should be taken away and bestowed in such

place, as the same should cause no superstition afterwards ~~as it is indeed amonges other of that sorte conveyed
and buryed in a noble towre~~[1]. And forasmuch as his head
almost whole was found with the rest of the bones closed
within the shrine, and that there was in that church a great
scoull (skull) of another head, but much greater, by the iii
quarter parts than that part which was lacking in the head
closed within the shrine, whereby it appeared that the
same was but a feigned fiction, if this head was brent, was
therefore S. Thomas brent? Assuredly it concludeth not.
St Swithan and other reliques where about abuse of hypocrisy was, be laid safe, and not as it is untruly surmitted
brent, but according to reason collocate secretly, where
there shall be no cause of superstition given by them, as
some say that for the like cause the body of Moyses was
hidden lest the Jews should fall to idolatry.

Not long after, another clerk of the Privy Council,
William Thomas, made a similar defence of King Henry's
proceedings. It was a more literary attempt than the former. Thomas spent much time in Italy, and had there
doubtless been confronted with disagreeable questions
about religion in England. He composed a not unskilful
dialogue called *Il Pellegrino Inglese*, which was published
in Italian in 1552, and after the author's death in English

[1] It has been suggested that the "tower" here mentioned and
erased was the whole eastern projection of the church, which was
built in St Thomas's honour. It is true that the chapels of St Anselm
and St Andrew are often called "towers." Perhaps at one time the
staircase turrets, which still remain, carried the beautiful Norman
towers which have since been removed to the eastern transepts, as
suggested by Prior Wibert's plan (cp. Willis, *Cathedral*, p. 140
*ad fin.*). The title might have been applied for a like reason to the
*Corona* chapel, but it would be an unnatural term to apply to the
whole of St Thomas's chapel. It is more probable that the writer
had in view an injunction like those relating to St Richard and St
Hugh (see above, pp. 126, 128) which ordered the delivery of relics
as well as shrines at the Tower of London. The words, it would seem,
were erased because it was remembered that St Thomas's relics had
been dealt with in another manner at Canterbury, as St Cuthbert's
were at Durham, and not "conveyed" with the jewels.

also. In this the "English Pilgrim" meets the objections of the Italian gentlemen with whom he falls in, and convinces them that the English king was justified in his action[1]. The portions of the dialogue with which we are concerned are here transcribed.

The objection is stated thus:

### THE PELEGRYNE.

(p. 74.)

The poore St Thomas of Canterburye, alas it sufficed hym not to spoyle and devour the great ryches of his shryne, whos treasure amounted to so manye thousand crownes: but to be avenged on the dead corpse dyd he not cause his bones openly to be burned? And consequently all the places where God by his saincte vouchsaffed to shew so many myracles, dyd he not cause them to be spoyled of their riches, juells, and ornaments and aft^d cleane destroyed?

This is the "Pelegryne's" answer:

And the pope remittyng both pena et culpa, taketh out of heaven and thrusteth[2] in to hell, and out of hell by the way of the[3] purgatory, carieth in to heauen, who it[4] pleaseth hym, placyng this Saint in the Queer of martirs, and that other amongst the virgins, confessors, and holy fathers, patriarchs and false prophetts, as he list to canonise

---

[1] The *Works of William Thomas* were published in 1774 by Abraham D'Aubant; the *Pilgrim* was separately republished by J. A. Froude in 1861. The English text here given is that of the British Museum MS. (Cotton, Vespasian D. xviii). This MS. is not, however, in Thomas's own handwriting, as Wordsworth, *Eccl. Biogr.* I. 569 (ed. 1863) says. There is a copy at Lambeth (no. 464) in the writing of Thomas James, the famous librarian of the Bodleian. The MS. from which he copied it is still in the Bodleian (no. 1972 Bernard), but Mr Craster kindly informs me that the hand cannot be that of W. Thomas. The MS. is all in one hand, and contains, besides the *Pilgrim*, some pieces of the dates 1547–1557; Mr Craster says that it is evidently the hand of a professional scribe of, he thinks, the middle of Elizabeth's reign. I give in the notes the readings of the Bodleian (B.) and Lambeth (L.) MSS.

[2] throweth (B.).          [3] his (B.).          [4] B. omits "it."

them, of which Canonisates, our S. Thomas of Canterbury is one: whose spoyled shryne and burned bones semeth so greately to offend your conscience: and it is true I cannot denye, butt that the kynges maiestie founde a wonderfull treasure aboute the same, for in the space of more then 250 yeres, I thinke there haue bene few kynges or prynces christened that dyd not either bryng or send, some of their richest jewels thether: and I reporte me unto you then, what the recourse of the common people was, to se that[1] Sepulchre, being so preciously adourned with Gold and stone, that at midnight you might in maner haue discryneth[2] all thinges as well as at nooneday. Butt now to speak of this Saints life and holynes in few wordes, I shall reherse unto you the effects[3] of his Story.

.    .    .    .    .

With the scornful recital we are not here concerned. It concludes thus:

These wordes were marked of them that wayted on[4] the Table, in such wise that with out more adoe, 7[5] of those Gentylmen waiters confederated[6] together, and streyght wayes toke their iourney to Canturbery, where tariyng there[7] tyme, on an euenyng fyndyng this Byshop in the Common Cloyster, after they had asked hym certayne questions, where unto he most arrogantly made answere, they slew hym. And here began the holynes: for incontinently as these gentylmen were departed, the monkes of that monastery locked up the Church doores, and perswaded the people that the bells fell on ryngyng by them selues, and there was crying of miracles, miracles[8], so earnestly that the deuillysh monks, to nourysh the supersticion of this new martired saynt, hauyng the place longe tyme seperate unto them selues, *quia propter sanguinem suspenduntur sacra*, corrupted the fresh water of a well there by, with a certayne mixture: that many tymes it

[1] † holie (B.), (L.).          [2] Discerned (B.).
[3] Effect (B.).                  [4] At (B., L.).
[5] 4 (B., L.).                   [6] Conferred (B., L.).
[7] Their (B.).                   [8] Om. second "miracles" (L.).

appeared bloudy, which they perswaded should procede
by Myracle of the holy marterdome: and the[1] water mer-
veylously cured all maner of infirmities, in so muche that
y[e] ignoraunt multitude came runnyng to gethers[2] of all
handes, specyally after the[3] false miracles were confirmed
by the popes canonisacion....

Butt the kynges maiestie that now is dead fyndyng the
maner of the[4] Saynts lyfe to agree evil[5] with the[6] proportion of a very sainte, and merveylyng at the vertue of this
water that healed all infirmities, as the blynde world[7] determined, to see the substanciall profe of this thinge[8], in
effect founde these miracles to be utterly false: for when the
supersticion was taken away from the ignoraunt multitude,
then ceassed all[9] y[e] vertue of this water, which now re-
mayneth playne water, as all other waters do: so that the
kyng moued of necessitie, could no lesse do then deface the
shryne that was Auther of so muche ydolatry. Whether the
doyng thereof hath bene the undoyng of the canonised saint
or not, I cannot tell. Butt this is true, that the[10] bones are
spred amongest the bones of so many dead men, that
without some great Miracle they wyll not be founde
agayne[11]. By my trouthe (sayde one of the Gentylmen) in
this your kyng dyd as I wolde haue done.

It may be doubted whether William Thomas had a first-
hand and independent knowledge of the facts; but he had
been trained in the traditions of Cromwell and was steeped

[1] This (B., L.).     [2] Thither (B., L.).     [3] That these (B., L.).
[4] This (B., L.).     [5] Ill (B., L.).     [6] Om. "the" (B., L.).
[7] † thought [above the line] (L.).     [8] † and (B., L.).
[9] Also (B., L.).     [10] His (B., L.).
[11] The corresponding Italian runs thus:
    Ma la Maiestà del Re hora morto, trouando la maniera dela vita
di questo Santarello malamente accordarse con la proportion d'vn
vero santo, & marauigliandosi de la virtù di quest' acqua, la quale
curaua tutte l' infirmita (come il cieco mondo credea) diterminò di
vedere la perfetta proua di tal cosa...Non so se la diffation di quella
sia stata la rouina ancora del Canonizato santo, ò si ò non. Ma questo
è ben vero, che le sue ossa sono sparse tra tante ossa di morti, che
senza qualche grã miracolo non si possono mai piu trouare.

in the official atmosphere of Henry's reign, and his virtual denial of the burning of the bones has more than ordinary significance.

Perhaps it is worth while to add here the words in which John Bale, writing in 1544, contrasted St Thomas with his hero of the moment, Sir John Oldcastle. Bale was not yet, in 1544, as he was afterwards, a canon of Canterbury, and had no special sources of information that we know of; but Cromwell was his patron, and his active mind was quick to take note of what was going on. He says:

SELECT WORKS OF BP. BALE.

(P.S., p. 58.)

When the gospel lay dead, glorious Thomas Becket was a saint, and John Oldcastle a forgotten heretic; but now that the light thereof shineth, we are like to see it far otherwise: for proud Becket hath already hidden his face, and poor Oldcastle beginneth now to appear very notable.... Such time as our most worthy sovereign King Henry the eighth, now living, after the most godly example of King Josias, visited the temples of his realm, he perceived the sinful shrine of this Becket to be unto his people a most pernicious evil, and therefore in the words of the Lord he utterly, among other, destroyed it. If he had upon that and such other abominable shrines brent those idolatrous priests which were (and are yet) their chief maintainers, he had fulfilled that godly history throughout. But that which was not then performed, in hope of their amendment, may by chance light upon them hereafter.

It would have suited Bale's purpose exactly to say that the king, like Josias, had burned men's bones at these shrines, if the king had in fact done so. But Bale, it is evident, had no knowledge of such a thing having taken place. The parallel with the Old Testament proceedings was not quite complete, and Bale a little ruefully suggests that the new Josias might have brought it nearer to completeness if he had only been less tender hearted to the idolaters.

# NOTE

## THE ALLEGED POSTHUMOUS TRIAL
## OF ST THOMAS

The confused way in which David Wilkins (*Concilia*, Vol. III. p. 835) has put together extracts from various authors in connexion with this subject, has caused a good deal of trouble. He quotes from three different authors, Nicholas Sander, *de Schism. Angl.*, Girolamo Pollini, *L'Historia ecclesiastica della Rivoluzion d' Inghilterra* (Rome, 1594), and Chrysostomo Henriquez, *Phoenix Reviviscens* (Brussels, 1626). As his manner too often is, he does not transcribe quite correctly the text which he had before him, nor does he show clearly where his quotations pass from one author to another. In regard to Sander, he fails to say what edition he is quoting from; and where the mention of Richard Hilliard (Eliardus) comes in, Wilkins does not make it clear which of his authors is referring to him. As a matter of fact, the words which Wilkins quotes as from Sander are only partly Sander's, being taken from Sander as re-edited by Persons. That Wilkins only knew Pollini's book through Henriquez, and not independently, would seem to be shown by a false reference taken over from Henriquez' margin (where "l. 3, cap. 42" is a mistake for "l. 1, cap. 42")—though Wilkins has correctly supplied (in modernized spelling) the title of Pollini's book. The facts of the case are these:

(1) The first edition of Sander's book was published after his death (he died in 1581) by Edward Rishton, at Cologne in 1585. The paragraph referring to St Thomas in this work is as follows:

Ac ne in illos tantùm qui agerent in terris sævire, in cælites autem nihil audere putaretur, *S. Thomam Beckettum* Cantuariensem Archiepiscopum, ab annis trecentis catalogo Sanctorum in cœlo ascriptum, atque infinitis miraculis illustratum, causam in terris dicere post tot secula coëgit, ipsumque perduellionis condemnatum, inter Divos ampliùs censeri vetuit. Imò in comitiis publicis sancivit, ut capitale crimen esset, si quis aut diem commemorationis eius sacrum celebraret, aut in sacris precibus mentionem eius faceret, aut omninò eum appellaret Sanctum nomenve ipsius in Calendario sanctorum non deletum remanere permitteret. Flagitium autem quod hic sanctissimus martyr commiserat ob quod adeò severè puniretur, nullum aliud fuit, quàm, quòd monumentum ipsius tantis opibus ac thesauris refertum erat, ut occasionem quæri oportuerit unde expilaretur. Qui enim Regius quæstor tunc erat, confessus est, tantam auri, argenti, ac lapidum preciosorum et sacrarum vestium vim ex uno illo D. Thomæ monumento ablatam esse, quanta viginti sex currus oneraverat, ut ex eo conjicere liceat quam innumerabiles thesauros ex cæteris Sanctorum monumentis, atque adeò ex templis, et monasteriis omnibus idem Rex corraserit.

Then follows an amusing story of a parish in Ireland where the church was dedicated to St Thomas, and was obliged to change its name.

(2) The work was immediately republished "locupletius et castigatius" at Rome in 1586. The enrichments and corrections were made by the famous Jesuit, Robert Persons, or Parsons[1]. They are contained in all the subsequent editions (Ingolstadt, 1588; Cologne, 1610, and 1628; etc.); and so form part of the foundation of books like those of Pollini and Henriquez. So completely does Pollini depend upon Sander as edited by Persons, that where Persons quotes a lamentation of Richard Hilliard on the subject of Henry's acts of sacrilege, and ends with "Haec ille," Pollini copies it out, "Haec ille" and all. Into the question of the relations between Sander-Persons and Hilliard, Pollini and Henriquez need never have been brought in at all. Though Pollini mentions "Ricardo Eliardo" in his margin, he has only copied the words from the margin of Sander-Persons, and had no first-hand acquaintance with Hilliard.

Persons, in republishing Sander's book, recast the passage about St Thomas, and greatly enlarged it. He introduced a paragraph about the three most celebrated of "English" martyrs, St Alban, St Edmund, and the martyred Archbishop, which was repeated by Pollini, Henriquez, and others. It begins: "Deinde ad tumulos martyrum progreditur, quos omnes expilabat, reliquiasque indignissimis modis tractabat." It ends with, "Quae omnia Henricus invasit ac diripuit, tanta feritate ac indignitate ut vir quidam doctus ac pius, qui sacri-

[1] See a paper by J. H. Pollen in the *English Historical Review*, Vol. VI. 1891, p. 42 foll.

legio interfuerat, his verbis de eo queratur." Then follows the lamentation above referred to, and in the margin "Richardi Hilliardi de Henrici sacrilegio querela."

When Persons says that Hilliard *interfuerat sacrilegio*, it is not to be supposed that he meant that Hilliard was an eye-witness of the process of destroying all the three shrines that he has mentioned, or of destroying any one of them. He only means that he was alive at the time and knew something of what was going on in England. It is this lamentation which ends with "Haec ille"; and the "Haec ille" seems to imply that the words which follow, "Henricus autem," etc., are neither taken from Hilliard, nor based on him. They are, in fact, a recasting of Sander's words given above, about Henry's special enmity to St Thomas; but they add nothing fresh about the summons of the saint to take his trial. They only repeat "causam iterum ad tribunal suum contumeliosissime dicere post tot secula coegit." And as I have said above, they add no-thing about the treatment of the relics, except that Persons proceeds to give, what Sander did not give, the bull in which Paul III accused him of burning them.

(3) The whole passage in Wilkins containing the king's citation of St Thomas and the sentence upon him are taken from Henriquez, and from no older authority. But in quoting them Wilkins makes Henriquez say what Henriquez does not say. Wilkins writes, "Haec sententia (ut refert F. Girol. Pollini, etc.)." Henriquez says "Haec sententia (quam refert Hier-onymus Pollinius)." There is a difference. Wilkins's *ut* implies that the subsequent passage is borrowed from Pollini, which it is not. Pollini only translates from Persons-Sander, "Citò adunque vituperosamente à comparire al suo tribunale per difendere nuovamente la sua causa," etc. He gives no form of citation to St Thomas, and no form of sentence passed upon him, but goes on (still following Persons) to the measures adopted by Paul III. Thus the "sententia quam refert H. Pollinius" of Henriquez means "the sentence (which Pollini refers to)." It does not imply, as Wilkins's "ut refert" would, that Pollini had recorded the citation and the sentence, but affirms that Henriquez is in a position to give the text of what Pollini had only mentioned in passing[1].

[1] Mr Pollen (*ut supra*, p. 45) has fallen into Wilkins's trap. Without having looked at Pollini for himself, he writes, "The

(4) The passage of Henriquez is as follows:

Haec sententia (quam refert Hieronymus Pollinius) scripta a rege et a senatu subscripta sic se habebat:

Henricus, Dei gratia Angliae, Franciae, et Hiberniae rex, defensor fidei, et ecclesiae Anglicanae supremum caput. Praesentium tenore citamus et vocamus ad supremum nostrum Consilium te Thomam, qui fuisti olim archiepiscopus Cantuariensis, ad agendum de mortis tuae causa, de scandalis, quae commisisti contra reges, nostros praecessores, et injusticia, qua tibi Martyris nomen arrogasti, quod potius ut rebellis et contumax contra regis tui et domini auctoritatem, quam ut fidem Catholicam propugnares, mortem subieris: quod[1] sine praejudicio ejusdem leges, quibus te opposuisti, quae dicere poterat, et esse supremus in rebus Ecclesiasticis judex, ut nos jam sumus. Et quia delicta tua commissa sunt contra regiam majestatem, quam hodie tenemus, citamus te ad audiendum sententiam. Et si non sit, qui pro te compareat, juridice procedetur, prout regnorum nostrorum leges disponunt et dictitant. Datum Londonii 24 Aprilis 1536 (sic)[2].

Henriquez continues:

Hanc male fundatam citationem jussit Henricus sancto viro ad sepulcrum significari per apparitorem publicum, et intimationis testimonium scribi. Et jam triginta dierum tempore illi statuto elapso lis contra sanctum scripto coepta, dato illi causidico, qui causam illius ageret, ut Rex volebat, et rationibus, quas volebat Rex, Henrici secundi actionem assumebat, et probare nitebatur, quod antiquae illae leges justae erant et is qui se eisdem opponeret, rebellis et contumax quodque illi, qui sanctum trucidarant, fidelium et bonorum subditorum munus implessent, utpote propugnantes Regis sui et Domini honorem et auctoritatem. Ex quibus omnibus secuta est saeva in S. Thomam sententia, Deo sic permittente, ut monstri hujus iniustitia et conatus impii tanto clariùs paterent, et S. Thomae memoria renouaretur in secundo suo martyrio. Sententiae tenor, ut refert Eliardus, erat, qui sequitur:

Henricus Dei gratia Angliae, Franciae, et Hiberniae rex, supremum ecclesiae Anglicanae caput, etc. Visa causa Thomae

warrants which Pollini professes to quote cannot be correct as they stand," etc.

[1] Wilkins upsets the sense by inserting a *non*, and other words.
[2] Wilkins has falsified the date.

quondam Archiepiscopi Cantuariensis, et quod coram nostro supremo Consilio citatus, nemo, qui causam ejus ageret, statuto termino comparuerit, et quod causidicus eı datus nihil allegeI in refutationem et rejectionem criminum rebellionis, contumaciae, laesae Majestatis, et proditionis contra Regem suum, ut poenam ipsis debitam effugeret: visa etiam probatione sufficiente omnium, de quibus accusatur, et quod vivens regnum turbarit, et totus in hoc fuerit, ut praedecessorum nostrorum regiam potentiam diminueret, quodque crimina ejus mortis causa fuerunt, et quod[1] ob Dei et ejus Ecclesiae honorem occubuerit, quod ejusdem superioritas pertinet ad hujus regni Reges, et non ad Episcopum Romanum, ut ille sustinebat in coronae nostrae praejudicium. Viso etiam quod populus eum habet pro Martyre, quod dicat eos, qui pro Ecclesiae Romanae authoritatis defensione mortem oppetunt, veneratione dignos esse. Ut ergo talium criminum rei puniantur et ignorantes errorem suum agnoscant, et abusus in regnum introductos fugiant: judicamus et decernimus dictum Thomam olim Archiepiscopum Cantuariensem ab hoc tempore non habendum pro sancto, nec Martyrem nominandum, nec inter justos ejus habendam mentionem, nomen et ejus imagines ex templis eradendas, nec eum in missalibus, precationum libris, calendariis vel litaniis nominandum, eumque ıncurrisse crimen laesae Majestatis, proditionis, perjurii et rebellionis. Et quia talis, mandamus ejus ossa ex sepulcro erui et publice comburi, ųt ex mortui punitione discant viventes leges nostras revereri, et nostrae se auctoritati non opponere. Aurum vero, argentum, lapillos pretiosos et alia dona, quae ad ejus sepulcrum simplices homines, quod eum sanctum crederent, quondam obtulerunt, tanquam bona ejus propria coronae nostrae confiscamus, ut regni hujus leges et consuetudo dictitat, et sub mortis poena et bonorum amissione vetamus, ne quis subditorum nostrorum eum ab hoc die sanctum nominet, nec ei preces legat, nec ejus reliquias secum ferat, vel ejus memoriam directe vel indirecte promoveat, nam tales eorum numero habebuntur, qui contra personam nostram regiam conspirant, vel cònspiratoribus favent et auxilium ferunt. Et ut nemo hujus edicti nostrı ignorantiam praetendat, jubemus ut idem in civitate nostra Londoniensi, Cantuariensi, et aliis regni nostri publicetur. Datum Londonii undecima die Junii 1538. Per Regem in suo Consilio.

[1] Wilkins again amends with a *non*.

After this, Henriquez pursues:

Proclamata hac iniqua et haeresibus plena sententia, jussit Rex edictum undecima die Augusti executioni mandari, et auferri omne aurum et argentum, quod ad sancti sepulcrum erat; tantaque ejus fuit quantitas, ut (teste Pollinio) viginti et sex magnis curribus vix avectum fuerit, et thesauris regiis illatum. Et decima nona ejusdem mensis die S. P. N. Bernardo sacra sacrilegium Regis jussu completum fuit, et venerandae S. Martyris reliquiae publice combustae, et cineres in ventum sparsi ut nulla ejus superesset memoria.

Wilkins's extract ends here, but we may as well give the remainder of the passage.

Populus, qui huic tragœdiae, intererat, tam Regis sævitiam et scelera est detestatus, ut dolorem celare non posset, et multis cum lacrymis proderet, sanctum rogans ut injuriam sibi illatam ulcisceretur, nec Ecclesiae honori, quam tam fortiter vivens defenderat, deesset. Sed ille quod præmio ex priore victoria parto jam frueretur, et Henricum secundum prostravisset moriens, et octavum post mortem esset ulturus, pœnam in. aliud magis oportunum tempus distulit, nec miracula, quae tam diu fecerat, occulto quodam Dei judicio sufflaminavit.

(5) It will be observed that Henriquez mentions "Eliardus," i.e. Richard Hilliard, as his authority for the terms of Henry VIII's sentence upon St Thomas. How did Henriquez come by such an authority? That Hilliard wrote a book on affairs in England is certain. Portions of it exist in manuscript in the British Museum (Arundel MSS. clii, 312, 313). There is no reason to think that it was ever printed until parts of it were published by Van Ortroy in his life of Bishop John Fisher (1893), extracted from the *Analecta Bollandiana*, Vols. x. and xII. It is of course conceivable that manuscript copies of the whole book or of parts of the book may have been in circulation and reached the hands of Henriquez, and that some such manuscript may have been "enriched" with the document which Henriquez ascribes to Hilliard. This would not prove that Hilliard himself was responsible for it. But it is hardly likely that Henriquez carried his researches so far, or that he was acquainted with Hilliard at first hand. It is more likely that seeing two references to "Ricardo Eliardo" in the margin of his Pollini, he assumed that "Eliardus" was the authority for all Pollini's information on the subject, and so ascribed to "Eliardu '

these documents which seemed to bear out the statements of Pollini. Whether Henriquez himself composed the documents, to suit the language of Pollini—that is, ultimately, of Paul III—or whether some ingenious person before him did the like, cannot now be proved. At any rate the documents do not now form part of the work of Hilliard preserved among the Arundel MSS.

But whatever may be discovered hereafter with regard to Hilliard and Pollini, the two documents which Henriquez has taken from them cannot be genuine as they stand. The following, among other reasons, have been pointed out by Froude, Stanley, Dixon, and others.

(1) Henry describes himself as *Hiberniae rex*, a title which he did not assume till 1542. Before that time he and his predecessors bore the title of *dominus Hiberniae*.

(2) Both documents are dated *Londonii*. Besides the unknown form of the name, such documents are never dated from London, but from Westminster, or St James's, or the Tower, or some other locality in London.

(3) The circumstantial setting of the second document, apparently so exact, is certainly wrong. It was not on St Bernard's day, August 19, that the shrine was despoiled and destroyed, but nearly a month later.

These facts are enough to awaken suspicion; and when it is added that there is no reference to any such procedure in the active correspondence between Cromwell and Prior Goldwell during those months—though it is part of the story that the citation was publicly affixed to the shrine—and that neither Pole in his declamations against Henry, nor any other contemporary English writer, alludes to any kind of trial of the saint—then we may well conclude that the whole story of the trial is a myth. I cannot agree with Dixon that the language of Paul III's bull of excommunication is not to be taken literally. Paul, I think, believed, or affected to believe, that Henry had cited St Thomas to appear in court and stand trial; and his bull persuaded many people to believe that this was so. But it was quite untrue—though not more untrue than many things believed or affirmed by popes about England from that time to this.

# SECTION IV

## THE SUPPOSED DISCOVERY OF THE BONES

# SECTION IV

## THE SUPPOSED DISCOVERY OF THE BONES

IT was on Monday, January 23, 1888, that the bones were discovered which give occasion to the foregoing investigations. The discovery was made in the course of researches undertaken for other purposes. The principal object was to ascertain the lines of the architecture of Lanfranc and of Ernulf in the eastern portion of the crypt of the church; but Mr C. F. Routledge, Mr W. A. Scott Robertson, and Dr J. B. Sheppard, had their eyes open for anything else that might be found. Their very brief report to the Dean and Chapter will be found in the *Archaeologia Cantiana*, Vol. XVIII. pp. 253–256.

After describing how they discovered, beneath the earth which was then piled on the floor, two steps fitted round the westernmost of the central vaulting shafts of the eastern crypt, which steps led to the altar of the Tomb of St Thomas, they say:

"About 4 feet west of the lower step, in a direct line (from east to west) with the central vaulting shafts, the narrow end, or foot, of a stone coffin was discovered. The coffin, which was 6 ft 2 ins. long[1], was broader at the west end than at the east. It was hewn out of a solid block of Portland oolite, and was covered with a thin slab of Merstham or Reigate fire-stone, utterly unfitted for such a purpose....

"When the above-mentioned stone coffin was examined, it was found to contain human bones, not placed in any regular order, but gathered together near the middle and upper portion of the coffin, and mingled with much earthen

---

[1] They do not say whether this was the inside measurement or the outside.

débris. No member of your Committee saw the coffin until the upper portion of the lid had been removed, if indeed the lid had remained complete until the time of this exploration.

"At the head of the coffin was a boulder-like stone, hollowed on its upper surface, as if to form a pillow. It had been broken across the middle.

"It was found that nearly all the bones of a complete human body were present in the heap. They were those of an adult of full stature, and of at least middle age. But there is no distinct evidence to show to whom they belonged."

The report is dated April 28th, 1888. The guarded nature of the last sentence is a tacit reference to the controversy, which began immediately after the discovery, as to whether the bones were those of St Thomas or not.

It is much to be regretted that fuller and more accurate notes were not taken at the time, that the bones were not photographed as they lay in the coffin, and that other eminent antiquaries were not called into consultation before the bones were moved. It is to be regretted also that the stone coffin was not itself raised, and the ground beneath it searched.

I have been fortunate in obtaining contemporary letters written by an eager and sympathetic eyewitness in the person of Miss Agnes Holland, afterwards Mrs Bolton, daughter of the Rev. Francis J. Holland, Canon Residentiary of the Cathedral. They were written to Miss Lisa Rawlinson, daughter of the Rev. George Rawlinson, who was also a Canon, but was then absent on his professorial duties at Oxford. They supplement the jejune account given in the report, and enable the reader to see what took place, as if with his own eyes.

# I.

(Between Jan. 25 and Feb. 4, 1888.)

I wish you were here more than ever. You can't think what an exciting week we have had of it. Last Monday the excavations were going on as usual in the crypt under Trinity Chapel, when they came upon a stone coffin exactly in the middle behind the Chapel of our Lady. It was only a few inches below the surface of the ground, and was covered by a broken lid. This was raised, and inside we found the skeleton of a man; but instead of being laid straight out, all the bones were laid together in the upper part of the coffin—the skull, which was in two or three pieces, lying by itself in a curious little hollowed stone cushion, which was likewise broken in half.

Austin[1] sent for the Bishop and the Dean[2], who came. My mother too was there and received the skull as it was taken out....[The bones] were gathered together and taken off to Austin's house....Austin got Mr Thornton—the doctor[3] —to come and arrange them. I have been again and again to see them there. I made a pall of thin white sarsnet silk with a broad edge of lace at either end, because I knew people would come to look and criticise, and so they have, and I am glad to say that Mr Waterfield[4] said he was very glad to see that proper care was being taken of the bones, and he kept murmuring, "Very nice; yes, this is all very nice." It was my Mother's idea, but we did not let any one know that we had made it....The bones look most curious and strange, lying there all arranged, with the skull set up straight over a clay mould at the neck. All

[1] Mr H. G. Austin, surveyor of the Cathedral, lived in the house which has since been incorporated into the Archbishop's Palace.
[2] Edward Parry, Bishop of Dover, and Robert Payne Smith.
[3] W. Pugin Thornton, nephew of the celebrated architect, A. W. N. Pugin.
[4] Of Nackington House.

the bones are there, save a piece of the skull on the left side of the head. The fracture begins on the top and extends all down the left side, and it was on the left side and shoulder that the blow was struck[1]. The corona is not cut off[2], but that may have been only the tradition, if this really is St Thomas of Canterbury.

Austin is convinced that it is,—

1. Because the Chronicle says the bones were not burnt, but buried[3]—

2. The bones were all at the top of the coffin, showing that they were placed there hastily—after the body had become a skeleton—

3. The coffin is most probably the very one—in the very place—in which the Saint lay temporarily[4]. It was known to be there, and what more likely than that the monks[5] should have put him there again?

4. There is no record of this coffin, though it lies in an honourable place.

Dr Shepherd[6] says "Piff paff," "All rubbish," and scouts the bare notion. But he evidently is at daggers drawn with Austin. He maintains that it is only one of several coffins which were brought in from the monks' cemetery[7]. He

[1] But see above, p. 49.

[2] This is perhaps a mistaken view of what was meant by corona; see p. 49.          [3] See p. 138.

[4] It is not clear what period the writer refers to. See p. 67.

[5] This assumes that the bones were buried by the monks rather than by order of the Commissioners.

[6] W. Brigstocke Shepherd, Seneschal of the Cathedral, the well-known editor of the *Litterae Cantuarienses*.

[7] It seems that when the earth was removed from outside the east end of the crypt, where the monastic cemetery lay, some human remains were carried into the crypt and buried there, but in what part of the crypt is not known. This must have been done at the time when the superfluous canonical houses and their gardens were done away with, about the year 1860; but unfortunately no record was kept, and I have been unable to find any one who remembers. The coffin, however, cannot have been brought in with these bones already in it—at least, they cannot have been originally buried in it, for the reason already stated—and the wound in the head would still require to be accounted for.

goes on to assert, which maddens Austin, that the skull has been fractured within the last fortnight, implying that Austin did it himself. I suppose we shall never know. I do not know what to think about it all, and find myself always agreeing with the last person, which is very weak, of course.

## II.

The Precincts, Feb. 4 [1888].

How I wish you were here to see all that is going on. In the first place you must really understand that it is not in the least out of curiosity that the two tombs have been opened. In the case of Bradwardine they only removed a few bricks from the head part to see if what Austin maintained was true—that it had been opened and was entirely empty[1]. They wanted also to know if it *was* a tomb. We think it is rather a pity that they began with Bradwardine, because it has made people think that the excavations have been only in search of tombs, which is quite contrary to all Canon Routledge's ideas or wishes. He began the excavations in the floor of the crypt only to see if he could find the foundations of the wall of Lanfranc's church. These were found yesterday while I was there, and very interesting they are—4 ft thick, just below the surface—and suddenly, to the surprise of all, came upon this stone coffin, lying close below the surface of the ground exactly in the middle of the space behind the Lady Chapel. Nine feet in front of it they have found the foundations of an altar, with two steps leading up to it. Behind this again, at the distance of 33 feet from the great pillars behind the Lady Chapel, is the outer wall of Lanfranc's church. The coffin lies therefore in a very honourable place. It is a rough one, which evidently did not belong to it [*sic*], and was broken a good deal.

It is impossible to say whether the bones are those of the saint or not; it never will be proved, I suppose. There is

[1] It was at once ascertained that the Archbishop's body was undisturbed.

no reason to reject entirely the idea with derision as some do, but on the other hand there is no real proof. The arguments for it are—

1. That all the bones are there except a piece on the left side of the skull, the fracture beginning from the top of the head and descending, enlarging as it goes, to the ear.

2. That the head is a splendid one, and the bones those of a tall man.

3. That the body was not originally laid in this coffin, because instead of being laid out straight out, [the bones] were all laid together in the upper part—rather as if they had been taken out of the chest and placed hurriedly here.

4. That the people who wished to bury the bones may very likely have thought of putting them back in the coffin which is probably the very one in which Becket was originally and temporarily laid.

5. The head and feet of a statue of an Archbishop in Purbeck marble have just been found in the crypt close to the tomb[1].

On the other hand people say that the monks would never have taken the bones out of the iron chest, or placed them there in the old place. That the lost piece is not the corona (which is quite true) and that as there is no real proof it is no use speculating, etc.

I cannot make up my mind to anything except that these are the bones of some distinguished and holy man. They are going to be carefully put in an oak chest and buried again immediately. Mr Routledge is very anxious for this to be done and certainly they have been above ground quite long enough. But they lie in an unused room, on some white deal boards, which are covered with grey cloth, and over the bones is a white silk pall, so that there is nothing irreverent to be seen, and everybody feels this.

I wish that the newspapers had not taken it up. Austin says that he has not a doubt that it is Becket, but he is the only person who asserts this as a fact....Dr Shepherd takes the other extreme and laughs at the idea. But we

[1] See *Archaeol. Cant.*, Vol. XVIII. p. 255.

shall never know:—it is only all very curious and interesting. A Jesuit, Father Morris of Farm Street, who has written a very good life of St Thomas of Canterbury, came down to see the bones. He is deeply interested, did not think that it was the saint—I suppose no Roman Catholic would think of allowing us to find such a treasure—but he said that he thought all had been done most carefully and reverently.

## III.

Precincts, February 10.

I am now going to finish the chapter of the finding of the bones.

All sorts of interesting things have happened this week. For instance, on Tuesday a gentleman came over from Margate, bringing with him his son. He asked to be allowed to see the bones, and then said that the boy's eyesight was failing, and that as he had tried all the doctors in vain, he had brought him as a last resource to see what the bones of the saint would do for him. Austin was delighted at this, and told us with great satisfaction how the gentleman made the boy kneel down and put his eyes close into the sockets of the skull, saying to him, "Now, no doctors can heal you; you must pray for yourself." Don't you hope that he will recover?....

Today we received the following from the Dean: "The bones will be replaced in the crypt at 3.30." And at 3.30 we were there, and just as I arrived the side door into the Innocents' Chapel[1] opened, and the little procession came in, Austin hurrying first, and then the two workmen bearing between them the bier covered with my thin white silken pall. I hastened to follow close behind, with my head and heart full of emotions, as you may imagine. They laid the bier down by the side of the rough open coffin, and

---

[1] Probably the door of the N.E. transept is meant, though at that time there were rough steps down through an unglazed window of the Holy Innocents' Chapel.

then proceeded to place in it (according to my father's suggestion) a very nice strong oak shell, which exactly fitted. Seeing what was coming, I took off the white silk covering and folded it and laid it in the coffin, the lace edge doubling over the curious hollowed stone pillow, which was replaced at the head. We thought [a Canon who was present] winced, but I felt as bold as brass. Austin let me do what I liked. Then Austin took the skull very carefully (still upon the clay mould) and laid it on the stone cushion, where I thought it looked more frowning and terrible than ever, and then Mr Thornton took his place, and receiving all the bones from Mr Austin laid them according to the latter's directions exactly in the position in which they were found, all neatly arranged in the upper part of the coffin. Does not this point to their having been taken out of a box or chest and laid thus? Then Austin took up a glass bottle in which a photograph of the skull and a careful record of the finding had been sealed up, and asked the Dean if he was quite satisfied, and the Dean hurried to say, "Oh yes," and then the bottle was solemnly laid behind the head, and then the lid of oak was quickly screwed down by Andrews[1], and we knew we had seen our last of the saint—for be he S. Thomas of Canterbury or not, he is some great and holy person. Then they cemented round the edge of the coffin and lowered down upon it a large new stone slab weighing 15 cwt. Then, I am sorry to say, the Dean assented to the proposition that the earth should be shovelled over it all again, and in five minutes every trace was hidden. But I heard Austin suggest that something should be laid upon it to prevent people from walking over it, and the Dean assented. I murmured softly in his ear, "Mr Dean, wouldn't it be very nice if something was made to mark out the place? Some pavement round you know, tiles or something?" "Oh yes. Something we will have..."

The photographs of the skull are beautiful and you will

[1] The foreman of the Cathedral workmen, to whose courage and skill in the fire of 1872 the preservation of the Cathedral is so largely due.

get a very clear idea from them of what it is like. But I do wish that you could have been here....

Did you see Fr Morris's letter in today's Times? He is quite wrong in supposing that the jaw was in the lower part of the coffin. Also it is impossible to say that the person whose bones these are could ever have been buried in this coffin. They are the bones of a man of 5 ft 11 in., and even little old Castle[1] could not get into the stone tomb. Andrews laughed at the notion that the coffin could have been tilted. The bones would have lain very differently if it had been.

IV.

Precincts, March 1.

I am going to answer your questions, but it will be rather *contre cœur*, because I can no longer believe that our Relics are those of St Thomas of Canterbury.

1. The coffin was discovered on the 23rd of January. I do not know at what hour precisely, but it was in the morning.

2. A pickaxe was the tool used.

3. Only Mr Austin and his men were present when the discovery was first made. Austin sent round word to the Dean and Canons in residence, and they all came in the afternoon. So did my mother, and she received the skull into her hands when it was taken out of the coffin.

4. They were all taken out by Austin and placed together in the first thing that came to hand, which happened to be an old box.

5. They were at Austin's house from the 23rd January to Friday February 10th, 3.30 p.m. Now they lie in the crypt again, with two gigantic blocks of stone [over them]. It is not a very sightly arrangement, but better than nothing.

Father Morris, who has been writing all those letters in

---

[1] One of the workmen. Mr Pugin Thornton in his little pamphlet *Becket's Bones* (1901) p. 4 says that he himself tried to lie down in the coffin, but his shoulders were too broad. Mr Thornton was under the middle height, though stoutly built.

the Times, has been down here twice, and came to lunch
with us. He is extremely interested in the whole affair.
He has poked and rummaged in among all the old MSS.
in the British Museum in the most indefatigable manner,
and has come at last to the conclusion, which I fear every
one will think decisive, that the bones were burned[1].
Harpsfield seems to have copied the old Chronicler wrong
in the first place, and every one since has copied him.
Father Morris has written an interesting article in the
"Month," which you must see. He says that he thinks the
bones may be those of S. Anselm, or of some other great
saint at Canterbury—so you see it is not from any petty
feeling of jealousy that he does not think that we have
found the Relics.

And I begin to feel very shaky about the wound in the
head. The photographs do not give a pleasing idea of the
bones, and one of them is ghastly.

At the risk of some repetition, it may be worth while to
add a letter written by the same lady to myself at a much
later time, in answer to enquiries, before the letters to
Miss Rawlinson had been recovered.

March 22, 1915.

I think I can remember pretty well all that happened,
for never in all my life have I been so much interested in
anything as in that tomb in the crypt.

1. Did I see the bones before they were touched? Yes.
I went immediately across to the Cathedral, and when I
arrived Mr Routledge and the workmen and Austin, I
think, were there. I stood with them and looked down into
the coffin. I perfectly remember the appearance of the
skeleton. The great head lay on the slightly raised, hol-
lowed-out, little stone pillow, and the bones were laid
round the head in a sort of square. It gave it a strange look.
One saw the teeth. While we were standing there, Dr
Parry, the Bishop of Dover, and others came in. My

[1] See p. 139.

father was there all the time. I remember distinctly that the bones were lying at that time exactly as we found them. ...Dr Shepherd, the Seneschal, arrived, and from the first he maintained that they were the bones of no one important. While we stood there, some one said, "Could they be the bones of St Thomas a Becket?" and then the question of the wound in the head was raised. And it was then that the slanting opening on one side of the skull was observed. And it was determined that the bones should be lifted out of the rough little coffin and submitted to a surgeon. I cannot remember if they were removed that very day. I know that Canon Routledge most carefully observed how the bones were laid, because I was there when he himself replaced them[1] in the shell which was put into the stone coffin when they were re-buried. Bone by bone, he laid them round the head, which once more reposed upon the stone pillow. Some who were there have said that a few small bones were lying upon the floor of the coffin. The coffin (it was more like a small trough) was not more than 3 inches below the earth, and its lid lay broken diagonally in two pieces on the floor of the crypt when I came in. At that time the crypt floor was only hard earth. I was always very sorry that they did not lift the coffin right out of the ground when the bones had been removed.

2. I am sure that there was not the slightest idea beforehand of finding the bones of St Thomas. Canon Routledge had been digging to see if he could discover the site of the first tomb in the crypt, and perhaps it may have been only a day or two before, that going down I had found him there alone with a workman, who was standing in a trench which he had dug a little to east or west of where the tomb was found. It was a deep trench, and he was splashing in water. I remember Canon Routledge telling me then that wherever one dug one came to the bog on which the Cathedral was built.

[1] This appears to be a small slip of memory. From the earlier letter on p. 180 it was Mr Thornton who replaced them.

3. I did not actually see the bones taken from the tomb. The next time I saw them was in a room in the Palace, where Dr P. Thornton was arranging them. He told my mother and me of the great height of the man whose bones they were, and how he could never have been laid in that tomb. The three striking things were—

A. The position of the tomb.
B. The arrangement of the bones.
C. The sword cut on the head.

A scientific account of the bones from Mr Pugin Thornton's pen, together with excellent photogravures, appears in *Archaeologia Cantiana*, Vol. XVIII. p. 257, immediately after the report above referred to. The main points in the account are these:

Five of the four and twenty vertebrae were missing, besides many pieces of other bones. Five teeth were in their places. A surgeon-dentist who was consulted judged from them that the age of the man to whom they belonged was about 50 years. This was confirmed by the character of the bones in general. Mr Thornton computed that the man in life must have stood about 6 ft 3 in. in height. The bones gave the idea of great strength. There was a fracture across what Mr Thornton calls "the crown of the skull," which he thinks had probably occurred during the removal of the bones from the crypt; one of the thigh bones had been broken in that process.

With regard to the right side of the skull he says that it "might have been fractured by a blow from a mace or pickaxe"—though he does not appear to think that this had been done recently, like the fracture in the top of the skull—"but not by a sword-cut."

More important is the evidence from the appearance of the other side of the head:

"On the left side, by far the greatest injury seems to have occurred. Here there was an aperture from 5 to 6 inches long, extending from a line drawn upwards from behind the position of the ear to the centre of the forehead. Besides

the loose pieces of bone, partly filling up this aperture,
there was another piece, about an inch broad and 1½ long,
not represented in our Plate, lying opposite the junction
of the frontal and left parietal bones. This unrepresented
piece of bone had a continuation of the coronal suture
marked upon it. Accordingly, if this be Thomas à Becket's
skull, no pieces of bone of any size could have been removed to be kept as relics.

"It is remarkable that the edge of bone which forms the
upper border of this aperture is almost in a straight line
for 5 or 6 inches, so that if this left side of the skull was
injured by force during lifetime, or after death, it is unlikely that it would have been done by a pickaxe or a
mallet, but it might have been caused by a heavy cutting
instrument, such as a two-handed sword.

"Extending from the upper edge of this aperture, there
is a crack in the skull about an inch and a half long, which
might have been caused during lifetime, inasmuch that it
only goes through the outer plate of the bone; and also,
had it been made after the bone of the skull had become
dry, it would have appeared, in all probability, as a rough
fracture[1]."

There are a few more facts to be stated which bear to
some degree upon the question whose bones these were.

### (1) *The locality where they were found.*

The eastern part of the crypt, where the bones lay, was
assigned in November 1546 to the stall of the First Prebendary, for domestic purposes.

---

[1] In talking to me—I think it was in 1896—Mr Thornton, who is
now dead, expressed himself more strongly about the main cut in the
head than he does in print, whether in the above report or in his
subsequent pamphlet *Becket's Bones*. He told me that he considered
it impossible that the great wound on the left side should have been
made after the skull was dry. A blow of such force falling upon a
dry skull must have broken it to pieces instead of shearing cleanly
through it.

186 THE LOCALITY

Willis, *Conventual Buildings*, p. 192.

The Bp. of Dovor, Dr Thorntons Lodging.

1. First to have ye vault called Bishop Becketts tombe under our Ladies chapell. The house called his bakehouse, his kitchen [etc.].

This portion was accordingly walled off from the rest of the crypt, and became the cellar of the house to which it belonged. So it presumably continued till the year 1864, when the house itself was ordered to be pulled down[1]. The bones therefore must have been placed, where they were found, either before 1546, or since 1864. They are not likely to have been buried there while "ye vault" was used for the Prebendary's wood or wine[2].

The "Bp of Dovor, Dr Thornton," to whom this cellar was first allotted, was a man of some note. He was professed a monk of Christ Church in the year 1512[3]. He attained the important position of Warden of the Manors of the convent[4]. Archbishop Cranmer had a high opinion of him, and wished him to be made Dean when the convent

[1] Chapter Minutes, Midsummer Audit, 1864.

[2] It is difficult to ascertain the date at which "Dick of Dover's" cellar was thrown open to the crypt again. Scott Robertson, *Crypt*, p. 55, writing in 1880, says that it was "in or about 1866," when the house of the Prebendary of the First Prebend was pulled down. He repeats the statement on p. 118. The year in which orders were given for pulling the house down was in fact 1864 as stated above. But living memories which go back to that date give the impression that the crypt was opened before then. The Antiquarian Report of 1888, signed by Scott Robertson himself among others, gives 1838 as the date; and Mr Morris, *Relics of St Thomas*, p. 14, gives the same. The Act for the suppression of canonries was passed in 1840. Two prints of the eastern crypt to be seen in the Beaney Institute and bearing the date 1841 seem to depict this part of the church as then still walled off. It was used for storing the stone for the contemplated completion of the Crown in the 'sixties. Most unfortunately the Chapter Minute book covering the period about 1838 cannot now be found.

[3] Searle, p. 194.

[4] Jenkins, *Remains of Cranmer*, I, 148, 238.

was dissolved. But Thornden (as he is more often called) did not remain constant to the cause which Cranmer had at heart. He was the man to whom Cranmer referred, when in his declaration after Mary's accession he wrote, "These be to signify to the world, that it was not I that did set up the Mass at Canterbury, but it was a false, flattering, lying, and dissimuling monk which caused Mass to be set up there, without mine advice or counsel. *Reddat illi Dominus in die illo*[1]." Under the name of "Dick of Dover" he gained an undesirable notoriety as a persecutor in the reign of Mary, and figures largely in Foxe. It would not be unnatural that a man of such character and history should contrive to gain possession of this portion of the crypt, if he knew that it contained a hidden treasure like the bones of St Thomas. No member of the convent was more likely to know.

(2) *The burial not necessarily furtive.*

It is usually assumed that if the bones of St Thomas were saved and buried when the shrine was destroyed, it must have been done by stealth, and at great risk, for fear of the wrath of the king[2]. This, however, is an unsafe assumption. It has been shown above that no special directions are known to have been given for the destruction of the genuine relics of St Thomas; and if there were no such directions, we should assume that the bones would be buried, secretly indeed, but under government authority. No doubt if any marked honours had been paid to the saint's memory by those who buried them, or if they had allowed the burying place to become publicly known and accessible to visitors, they would have drawn down punishment upon themselves. This was the thing which the government was bent on preventing. But so long as the thing was done quietly, and nothing was said which would

[1] Jenkins, IV. 2.
[2] This, for instance, forms a main consideration in the deeply interesting Essay of my dear friend the late Dr E. Moore on *The Tomb of Dante*, with Appendices, in the Fourth Series of his *Studies in Dante*.

give a clue to their hiding place, the burial could be done without great anxiety. This, as we have seen, was the procedure at Durham. The Chancellor of Lincoln Minster, Dr Johnston, informs me that not long ago an intelligent workman, now living, came upon a headless skeleton buried in the middle of the narthex of the Chapterhouse. He thinks it probable that this was the skeleton of St Hugh, whose head is known to have been kept separate from the body. We have no need, therefore, to imagine that the monks furtively extracted St Thomas's bones from the shrine, to substitute others for them, before the Commissioners came, or that in any other way the royal injunctions were evaded. Prosaic as it may seem, the convent probably allowed the Commissioners to find the bones untouched, and to burn the spurious relics which were duplicates of those contained in the shrine, and proceeded to dispose of the genuine relics in the way that the Commissioners enjoined. Richard Thornden may very well have been one of those complacent "monkes and chief officers of Christchurch in Canterbury," who "travelled abowte the disgarnisshinge of" the shrine "and other thinges there," and received payment from Wriothesley for their services. These men knew better than to divulge the secret. The world was only to be informed that the bones were "collocate secretly," where "no cause of superstition" should be given by them.

### (3) *The stature of the bones.*

Mr Thornton's opinion was that the bones were those of a man of about 6 ft 3 in. in height. His estimate was perhaps excessive. That St Thomas was a tall man we are assured on the unimpeachable evidence of William Fitzstephen, who knew him well. Fitzstephen says:

Erat siquidem placido vultu et venusto, statura procerus, naso eminentiore et parum inflexo[1].

Later tradition exaggerated the saint's height to that of a giant. A fragment preserved in a MS. at Lambeth contains a table of the "longitude" of various personages

[1] *Materials*, III. p. 17.

in history. Moses measured "xiij fote & viij ynches & di."
"Seynt Thomas of Caunterbery" measured "vij fote save
a ynche[1]." Stanley speaks of the length of the vestments,
said to have been his, at Sens, and relates how the tallest
priest was selected to wear them on the days when they
were used, and how even so they needed to be pinned up[2].
But more moderate accounts also found their way into
tradition. There is a fragmentary Thomas-Saga quoted by
Magnússon which says:

"He was of rather tall middle stature, courteous, dark
of hair, with a rather long nose, straight faced[3]."

There is nothing in the "longitude" of the Canterbury
bones which would forbid us to believe that they are
St Thomas's. They would at least suit the account given
by Fitzstephen.

### (4) *William of Andeville*.

If we suppose that these bones were deposited in the
crypt *before* 1546, and yet are not those of St Thomas, a
known claimant comes in view. Mr William Pugh, formerly
Head Vesturer of the Cathedral, a venerable man of acute
mind and fond of research, recalled to notice that a certain
William de Andeville, Abbot of Evesham, was buried on
that spot in 1159. He maintained that the bones must be
those of William de Andeville. Mr M. Beazeley (*The
Canterbury Bones*, p. 35) has followed Mr Pugh in this
attribution, as he has followed Mr Pollen in identifying
Charles Wriothesley the chronicler with Thomas Wriothesley the commissioner. That William de Andeville,
who had formerly belonged to our convent, was buried
there is certain. The Chronicle of Evesham (Rolls Series,
p. 99) says:

Huic successit Willielmus de Andevilla, monachus Christi
ecclesiae Cantuariae, ubi jacet sepultus ad Caput Thomae
martyris, qui, antequam illuc iret causa visitationis, quando

---

[1] *Three Fifteenth Century Chronicles*, Camden Society, 1880, p. xxvii.
[2] *Memorials*, p. 196.                    [3] Vol. ii. p. lvii.

ibi a Domino est visitatus, vidit in somnis, sicut fratribus retulit, quod sol sepultus erat ad pedes ejus. Quae visio interpretationem accepit processu temporis, postquam beatus Thomas sepultus est ad pedes ejus.

But if the bones under discussion are those of the Abbot of Evesham, one thing is certain: when found in 1888, they had not lain untouched since their burial in 1159. They were too long for the coffin that they were found in. They had been grouped, as bones, in one part of the coffin. Some of the bones were missing. There was no trace of any clothing, such as the Abbot must have been buried in, nor of chalice or paten or staff, such as he would be likely to have had. It is also hardly credible that the coffin in which the Abbot was placed came so close to the floor of the crypt, within three inches of the surface of the ground. The slab which covered it was not such as was likely to have been used for the Abbot's burial. The slab was broken—though at what period is uncertain—and earthy débris had fallen into the coffin. If therefore the bones were Abbot William's, they had been shifted at some time, after the resolution of the body and its clothing, into another and an improper receptacle, though buried again at the original place. We are left to ask when and why. And, as Dr Moore asks[1], "Above all, why should the Abbot have a deep cut in his skull"—and a deep cut inflicted before or soon after death?

Mrs Bolton in her letter of March 22, 1915, regrets that the coffin was not lifted right out of the ground. If this had been done, perhaps the Abbot's own coffin might have been found beneath it. Supposing however that the Abbot's coffin is not still there, or that this ill adapted receptacle *is* his coffin, it is perhaps more likely that the Abbot should have been ejected from his place, to make way for bones of greater eminence, than that his remains should have been disturbed, rearranged, and left *in situ*—and this, presumably, before 1546.

[1] *Ut sup.* p. 200.

(5) *The Shrine not re-erected*.

The argument has been frequently repeated, that if the bones of St Thomas had been known still to exist, the shrine would have been re-erected when Mary came to the throne.

To this argument it is sufficient to reply that things in history are not always what might *a priori* have been expected. Mary and her government were not as systematic and thorough in their reaction as a modern doctrinaire might have wished. In this particular field of action we are not left to conjecture: we know what they did and what they did not. It was known, though only to a few, where the relics of St Cuthbert and St Bede at Durham lay: what effort was made to restore their shrines? It was known where the bones of St William lay at York: what effort was made to bring them out again? There must have been similar cases elsewhere. Was any shrine in England restored, besides that of St Edward at Westminster? The shrine of St Frideswide at Oxford may perhaps be considered a second—but the fabric of the shrine there does not appear to have ever been demolished, though St Frideswide is said to have been dislodged, and the wife of Peter Martyr put in her place and then turned out again to readmit her, and finally herself readmitted to rest beside her. There is therefore nothing to be surprised at if the bones of St Thomas were known to be in Bishop Thornden's cellar, and left there.

### CONCLUSION.

The bones discovered in 1888 are those of a man corresponding in age and height to what is known of St Thomas —and of a man who appears to have been killed by a blow on the left side of the head from a sharp edged weapon. They had been removed from elsewhere to the place where they were found, and presumably before the year 1546. The size of the stone coffin, and the condition in which the bones were discovered, show that this was not where they

were deposited at death. Unless they were known to be
the bones of some one of importance, they would not have
been thus moved, and to that spot.

If at the time of the martyrdom a large part of St Thomas's skull was severed from the rest, then this is not the
head of St Thomas. But the historical evidence concerning
St Thomas's death-wound or wounds is conflicting. Though
it was early believed that the tonsured part of his head was
severed, and though something which was supposed to be
this tonsured part—the corona—was kept separate from
the shrine, beginning at a period within fifty years of his
death, it is by no means certain that this relic was genuine.
None of the first-hand witnesses records the separate preservation of such a relic. The most detailed account of the
damaged head—that of Gervase—does not suggest such
an amputation, and might well be read as a description of
the head discovered in 1888. Some small bones (*ossicula*)
were removed from the coffin at the time of the Translation,
but the corona cannot have been reckoned among these,
and at no other time was the coffin opened until the demolition of the shrine. Though some allowance must be
made for polemical interest in the account of the contents
of the shrine given by the agents of Henry VIII's government, if that account is at all true, the reputed *corona*
or "head" cannot have been genuine.

It was popularly believed, at home and abroad, that the
contents of the shrine were burned by Cromwell or by his
orders. But there is no direct evidence that this was the
case. It was not the usual mode of dealing with the bones
of canonized persons. There is no documentary evidence
that St Thomas's bones were ordered to be treated differently from those of other saints. When the report that his
bones had been burned began to give trouble, the official
reply was promptly given that they had been "taken away
and bestowed in such place as the same should cause no
superstition afterward," and that what was burnt was a
"feigned fiction," viz. the "great skull of another head,"
kept in a separate reliquary. The burning of this spurious

but venerated relic was quite sufficient to give rise to the belief that the bones of St Thomas had been burned.

Meanwhile there was no place more suitable to bury the bones of St Thomas in than the spot where the bones of 1888 were found. There they would be "hidden honestly away" in a place where the public would not have access to them, and without any mark to show what they were. To imagine that such a burial would require to be done by the monks furtively, in order to elude the vigilance of Cromwell and his agents, is altogether superfluous. If done, it was done under Cromwell's direction, like the burial of St Cuthbert at Durham. That the relics, if such they are, were not brought out again in the reign of Mary is no more surprising than in the case of St Cuthbert.

These facts seem to point to the conclusion that the bones in question are the bones of the great Archbishop. If they are not, the most probable conjecture would be that they are the bones of St Alphege, with his head cloven by the Danish axe[1].

[1] I owe this suggestion to my brother, the Rev. G. E. Mason, until lately Principal of St Bede's College, Umtata.

# INDEX